Will Our Children
Have Faith?

Will Our Children Have Faith?

John H. Westerhoff III

Third Revised Edition

Morehouse Publishing
NEW YORK · HARRISBURG · DENVER

First published in 1976 by Seabury Press.

Revised and expanded edition copyright © 2000 by John H. Westerhoff III

Third Revised Edition copyright © 2012 by John H. Westerhoff III

Morehouse Publishing, 4775 Linglestown Road, Harrisburg, PA 17112

Morehouse Publishing, 445 Fifth Avenue, New York, NY 10016

Morehouse Publishing is an imprint of Church Publishing Incorporated.
www.churchpublishing.org

Cover design by Laurie Klein Westhafer
Typeset by Denise Hoff

A catalog record of this book is available from the Library of Congress.

ISBN-13: 978-0-8192-2800-0 (pbk.)
ISBN-13: 978-0-8192-2801-7 (ebook)

Printed in the United States of America

Dedicated

to

Caroline, my wife,

and

our children and grandchildren.

Contents

Preface to the Second Edition

To appreciate, understand, or make use of a book's content, it helps to know something about both the author and the historical, social context in which it was written. In this new preface to *Will Our Children Have Faith?* I would like to share my story and my reading of the times in which I wrote it.

I was born on June 28, 1933, in Paterson, New Jersey. My maternal grandfather was a practicing Roman Catholic who died just before my mother was born. My grandmother, a Protestant by birth and an agnostic by conviction, brought my mother up to respect and appreciate every religion. Not being raised in a particular tradition, my mother accompanied her friends to Roman Catholic and Protestant churches as well as Jewish synagogues. My father's mother and father were Dutch immigrants who had been born into the Reformed Church in the Netherlands but had no church affiliation in this country, so neither did my father. Nevertheless, four months after my birth I was baptized at the Presbyterian Church in which my parents had been married.

When I was three my mother took me, for about a year, to Sunday school in that same church. But the church was distant from where we lived and we stopped attending.

When I was eight, a neighbor offered to take me to her church, a nondenominational, fundamentalist congregation. Every Sunday evening I went with her to a revival meeting. I participated fully, and the assistant pastor took a liking to me. We would talk together after the service, and one day he came to visit my mother. He told her that he was sure that God had called me to be a minister of the Gospel and that she should encourage me to hold revival meetings in our garage for the children of our neighborhood. My mother was so upset by his visit that she refused to permit me to attend that church again. Shortly thereafter we moved.

By the time I was thirteen, I was able to make my own decisions about how I would spend Sunday mornings. One Sunday I wandered up the street from our home and entered a Community Church that, to my pleasure, I discovered was related to the Dutch Reformed Church. Soon I was befriended by the pastor, a learned man with a doctorate in Calvinist theology. I was convinced that there was only one truth and that my authority, the Bible (interpreted by the pastor, Dr. Vernon Oggell), had it. He too told me that I was destined to be a minister, encouraged me to take a leadership role in worship each week, and gave me my own Sunday school class to teach. He was my father in God, and I followed him around like his own son. What is important for me now is that I was not brought up in the church by believing parents. I was a convert whose beginnings were in the Reformed, Calvinist, evangelical, intellectual tradition, a tradition I still appreciate.

Following high school I attended Ursinus College in Collegeville, Pennsylvania, a college in the evangelical and Reformed (now United Church of Christ) tradition. Still committed to becoming a minister (my nickname was "Preach"), I went through a period of questioning and searching. I became convinced that there was no one truth, only the truth each person holds. I had my own truth, and I was committed to convincing conservative, evangelical Christians that theirs was wrong. I refused to attend the local church because I believed the pastor was ignorant and misinformed about Scripture.

Instead, I organized my own congregation, led its worship, and taught a class for about twenty other questioning students at the college. In those days I was arrogant and self-righteous. I chose to have no connection to any institutionalized Christian tradition. But I prayed regularly and read every book on Scripture and theology I could find.

My next stop was the Harvard University Divinity School. All that I was sure of was that I was called to be an ordained minister in the church and needed to study theology. Importantly, during those three years I was formed as a Christian, a pastor, and a teacher in the church. For me, these remain the most significant and trans-forming years of my life.

My Harvard experience had two dimensions. The first was academic and was the consequence of friendships I formed with a number of the faculty: a Russian Orthodox priest and professor of church history, Georges Florovsky; a Roman Catholic histo-rian, Christopher Dawson; a Lutheran New Testament professor and pastor, Krister Stendahl; a Lutheran professor, theologian, and pastor, Paul Tillich; a Unitarian ethicist and pastor, James Luther Adams; a United Church of Christ New Testament scholar, Amos Wilder; and an Anglican professor of Greek and Roman religion, Arthur Darby Noch.

These relationships influenced my life in numerous ways. Intellectually I came to the place where I was able to acknowl-edge various possible truths, and choose one that I could believe and advocate, while remaining open to others. I became convinced that truth is found when two opposite propositions are held in ten-sion. Heresy occurs when one of the propositions is affirmed and the other denied. But more importantly I learned that there are two ways to think and know, the intellectual and the intuitive. And it is the intuitive, the pre-rational, nurtured and expressed through the arts, that is foundational to religious life. I also learned that people don't really learn unless they are passionately searching.

This learning also requires that someone be willing to let his or her life be a resource to the searcher. Any truth that is revealed, is revealed to them both.

The second dimension of my life at Harvard was related to finding a Christian tradition in which I could be at home and be formed as a pastor and teacher. I needed a job to help pay my way through Harvard, and I was hired to direct the youth ministry of the First Congregational Church (United Church of Christ) in Needham, Massachusetts. Here a new "father in God" emerged. Herbert Smith, trained at Harvard as a lawyer, had a doctorate in divinity and was the pastor of this congregation. He became my dearest friend and mentor, the single most influential person in my life. He understood himself as the church's teacher. His sermons were written lectures and his lectures read like sermons. He read and studied for four hours each morning. He never let an opportunity go by, whether in a formal or informal setting, to engage people in learning. He focused his efforts on adults, believing that they were the keys to a healthy educational ministry. Worship (he was a high church, Eucharist-every-Sunday Congregationalist) and nurture were the foundations of his ministry. He invited me to share in this ministry and then took the time to reflect with me each week on my experiences. In 1958 I was ordained in this congregation and accepted my first call.

My first parish was in Presque Isle, Maine. The people there also formed me. No one ever called me, even for a death, before noon because they believed I should be studying. And they would comment on some Sundays, "Well-studied sermon, pastor." They joined me for Morning Prayer each day and attended my adult class in large numbers. At the time, the United Church of Christ was publishing a new church school curriculum resource. I believed, and still believe, that it was among the finest ever produced. I proceeded to enlist faithful adults as teachers and provide them teacher education and support. We redesigned and redecorated our church school rooms and secured the latest audio-visual equipment. I was confident that we could develop a quality program of Christian education.

I took this enthusiasm with me when two years later I returned to Needham, Massachusetts, to oversee an educational program for more than two thousand persons, half of whom were children and youth. Working with me were a professionally trained director of children's ministry and a director of youth ministries. I focused on adults. We developed what in its day was considered an exemplary church school program. Nevertheless, I soon faced two unexpected realizations. First, I became aware that the informal "hidden curriculum" of life in this congregation was far more significant and influential than our formal educational program. Second, I became aware that on those special occasions when we gathered as an intergenerational group for worship or some other program, learning appeared to be more engaging and vital. I also learned that education takes place in a particular historical, social, cultural, and denominational context and that no educational resource, model, or structure was equally useful in every congregation. Further, I discovered that the learning needs of people do not always correspond to a schooling context, an instructional design, or curriculum resource.

After four years I left for the First Congregational Church (U.C.C.) on the campus of Williams College in Williamstown, Massachusetts, with more questions than answers, but with one conviction: adult education would be the most important aspect of my ministry. I was convinced that unless we could transform and form the lives of adults and reform the life of a congregation, our other educational efforts would have limited influence. Believing that education was still the way to accomplish this transformation, we developed imaginative programs with adults. I met with physicians in the hospital, the college faculty in the faculty club, businessmen and women in the Williams Inn, and parents in their homes. The process we followed was simple: we shared various aspects of our lives; we explored our Christian tradition; we reflected on the dissonance between this tradition and our lives; and we sought to resolve the dissonance with a commitment to a new way of life.

We also experimented with ways to improve our church school by focusing on the relationships between teachers and pupils. We designed opportunities for learning in our choirs and other groups of the church as well as in family clusters. Further, we improved baptismal, confirmation, and marriage preparation. But most important, we stopped having the church school for children and youth meet at the same time as worship. We all studied at the same time, making possible a new program for adults, and we all worshipped together. Before I left (the year was 1966) we had not evaluated any of these interventions, but we had experienced a great deal of enthusiasm for learning.

I had been in the parish eight years, and I had received a call to join the staff of the United Church Board for Homeland Ministries to develop a new magazine on issues of education in church and society. A year later "Colloquy" was born. For the next eight years it was my job to have new experiences and reflect on them, to ask foundational questions and explore alternatives, to state problems and seek solutions. I traveled around the world and interviewed almost every significant person in the field of church and secular education. These years corresponded with an era of turmoil, conflict, and change in the United States and the church, years in which I was on the liberal, progressive extreme of politics but had begun to form new friendships with Roman Catholics of the same convictions. I became increasingly troubled by our educational efforts. I wrote *Values for Tomorrow's Children,* my first book, in 1971 to express my concerns and suggest alternatives.

At the close of this period I completed a doctorate in the foundations of education at Teachers College, Columbia University, and

Union Theological Seminary. I studied with friends and colleagues, who encouraged me to bring together my thoughts on Christian education, thoughts that I began to publish and test. I soon became established, to my dismay, as an original, somewhat controversial new voice in the field of Christian education. Once again, experiences and particular persons influenced me. At Union it was Robert Lynn and C. Ellis Nelson in religion and education. At Columbia it was Phil Phenix in philosophy, Lawrence Cremin in history, Dwayne Huebner in curriculum theory, and most important for my later thought, a group of cultural anthropologists: Margaret Mead, Clifford Gertz, Victor Turner, and Lambros Comitas. My thesis was entitled *McGuffey and His Readers: Piety, Morality and Education in 19th Century America.*

Convinced that if the church was to make any significant change in its educational ministry we had to influence the clerical leadership of the church, after one year at Harvard, I accepted an invitation to join the faculty of the Duke University Divinity School as an assistant professor of religious education. It was there that I began to articulate the problems of Christian education as I understood them and offer possible solutions. *Will Our Children Have Faith?*, written in 1976, was my first and perhaps most significant effort. All my other books either prepared me for writing it or have been in some sense commentaries on or expansions of thoughts in this seminal book. It was translated into numerous languages and sold thousands of copies. Soon after it went out of print I began to receive letters from lay persons, clergy, teachers, and scholars suggesting I find a way to make it available again. Michael Warren, one of my dearest friends, who teaches at a Roman Catholic school of theology, finally convinced me that it was still relevant and useful. I am, therefore, deeply grateful to Morehouse Publishing for being willing both to reprint it and permit me to bring it up to date.

My twenty years at Duke were both formative and productive. Hundreds of articles and chapters in books accompanied the many books I wrote during those years. They are mostly out of print (see the appendix). Each was intended to be a tract for our times. I never tried to create a system or definitive work. I wrote books like painters paint paintings. I began with some specific issue, question, or problem. I tried to resolve it through lectures and the responses people made to them. I then wrote the book and sent it off to a publisher. I have rarely reread one of them, mainly because I was already drawn to something new to explore.

Two important learnings for me occurred at Duke. The first was the discipline of practical or pastoral theology that asks the question, "How are we who are believers in Jesus Christ and members of his church to live?" needed to be reestablished. Once, this discipline had six dimensions: liturgies (including homiletics), ethics, spirituality, pastoral care, catechetics (education), and ecumenics (mission and ministry, including stewardship and evangelism). Then ethics and ecumenics were consumed by systematic theology, and spirituality was forgotten. Pastoral care was modeled after secular psychology, and education after secular education. Church administration was added, which turned stewardship into church finance and evangelism into church growth. More serious, they were each turned into a separate field of study. Worse, each of these separated fields was expected to provide only "how to" courses in the service of Scripture, church history, and systematic theology. I soon became convinced that these separated fields of study needed to be reunited as a theological and theoretical/practical discipline. I ended my work at Duke as Professor of Theology and Christian Nurture, and there was an "and" in the title of every course I taught.

My second learning at Duke was that catechesis, or christening, the means by which persons and communities are shaped or formed to be Christian, was multidimensional, but liturgy or ritual was the key that held the pieces together. It was that conclusion, nurtured by friendship with Roman Catholic and Orthodox church educators, that first attracted me to the Episcopal Church, a part of the

Anglican Communion that believes that orthodoxy is right worship and that the rule of prayer is the rule of believing. But there was more. I was always torn between being a Roman Catholic and a Protestant, and the Anglican Communion, committed to being a bridge, embracing both of their understandings of the Christian faith and life, made a happy home. And so, soon after I went to Duke, I became a priest in the Episcopal Church. I did not leave the United Church of Christ for any negative reasons, but I needed to embrace the Roman Catholic in me. Also convinced that no one can teach what he or she is not practicing, I became a priest associate at the Chapel of the Cross, an Episcopal parish on the campus of the University of North Carolina. In my last years at Duke I lived in and participated in the life of a monastic community at St. John's House, founded by the Anglican men's religious order, The Society of St. John the Evangelist.

Then, after twenty happy, productive years at Duke, I discerned that God wanted me to return to the parish, my first love, so I left the school. My identity had never been as an academic scholar or professional Christian educator. I was a priest, a pastor, and teacher. After a year as interim rector at St. Bartholomew's Church in Atlanta, Georgia, I joined the staff of St. Luke's in Atlanta as a theologian-in-residence and the founding director of the Institute for Pastoral Studies, a cover for me to teach and write while being fully involved in the parish as a priest. Just before I moved to Atlanta I married Caroline Hughes, a lay Canon to the Episcopal bishop of Atlanta for Congregational Life and Ministry. We had written *On the Threshold of God's Future* together. Caroline continues to stretch and inspire me. Her books *Calling: A Song for the Baptized* and *Good Fences: The Boundaries of Hospitality* have influenced me greatly. The person I am today I owe to our life together. I will always be extremely grateful.

I hope it is now obvious that my thoughts, convictions, and commitments are a consequence of my history and how I responded to various relationships, experiences, and influences along the way. They have not significantly changed since I wrote *Will Our Children Have Faith?* but they have been refined and expanded. I remain convinced that the schooling, instructional-training paradigm is inadequate. A catechetical, community of faith/body of Christ paradigm is more faithful. Catechesis includes instruction and training; however, formation, a concept that has become popular but has not yet been clearly defined, is the essential element. In the Afterword I will explain this. Nevertheless, education remains the key to faithful intentional formation. In the notes following each chapter and in the Afterword I have tried to reveal some of the ways my mind has grown over the years and how I now understand the process by which persons and communities are enabled to be Christ-like.

I am grateful to you who have chosen to read this early work for the first time and to you who will read it again after many years. I remain humbled by the fact that anyone is helped by my attempts to reflect upon my experiences, and so I thank you!

CHAPTER ONE

The Shaking of the Foundations

The immediate future of liberal Protestant education is uncertain. Despite its appearance of modernity and relentless relevance, mainstream Protestantism is rooted in the ethos of the last century. [The issue that faces us is] do we have the courage to acknowledge the shaking of the foundations?

Robert W. Lynn

It is a truism that Christian faith and education are inevitable companions. Wherever living faith exists, there is a community endeavoring to know, understand, live, and witness to that faith. Still, an accurate description of education in the church today is difficult. Here and there exemplary educational ministries flourish, but in many more places anxiety, confusion, frustration, despair, and even failure exist. While generalizations may be difficult, few would defend the contemporary health and vitality of Christian education

within mainline Protestant Churches. Since 1957 when *Life* magazine dubbed the Sunday school the most wasted hour of the week,
increasing numbers of church persons have admitted that their educational ministries are less than adequate for the day. The church
school, despite numerous bold innovations and even a few modern
success stories, is plagued with disease. There may be disagreement over the severity of the illness and the prognosis of recovery,
but there is no debate as to whether or not all is well. Differing
diagnoses, however, do exist. For example, it appears that many
church educators are sure that we are dealing with a surface infec-
tion, while I am convinced that we face a very serious disease.

   This conviction is not entirely new. *Colloquy* (an ecumenical
magazine on education in church and society) was born in 1968
and for eight years, as founder and editor, I advocated the need for
radical change in church education. In 1970, just before the walls
of mainline Protestant church education began to show its cracks,
I published a series of works which boldly suggested that an alternative for church education was needed. I have now concluded that
it is not enough simply to conceive of alternative programs for
church education; fundamental issues once clearly resolved need to
be explored afresh. No longer can we assume that the educational
understandings that have informed us, or the theological foundations that have undergirded our efforts, are adequate for the future.
A continuing myopic concern for education, understood primarily
as schooling and instruction and undergirded by increasingly vague
pluralistic theologies, will not be adequate for framing the future
of religious education. Today we face an extremely radical problem
which only revolution can address. We must now squarely face the
fundamental question: Will our children have faith?

BEGINNINGS

The roots of our problem go back to the turn of the century and a joke: "When is a school not a school?" The answer: "When it is a Sunday school!" Coming when it did, this characteristic comment triggered a reaction throughout mainline Protestantism. A new generation of leaders, in what was commonly referred to as religious education, emerged. They were embarrassed by the Sunday school and impressed by the emerging public school system with new understandings of child development and pedagogy. The Sunday school, they believed, was outmoded and needed to be replaced. The times, they concluded, called for both the birth of a new church school (modeled after the public schools) and the introduction of religious instruction into the nation's common schools. Thus in 1903 the Religious Education Association was founded with the dual purposes of inspiring the religious forces of our country with an educational ideal and the educational forces with a religious one.

The church school envisioned by these women and men of the progressive era conformed to an image of the best in public education. A new profession was born to create and sustain the church school. Seminaries developed departments of religious education and conferred degrees, directors and ministers of religious education were employed by the churches, and denominations responded with a new educational bureaucracy. The old-time people's Sunday school had begun to be transformed into the professional's church school. Soon religious education, influenced by liberal theology, was identified with church schooling and the instruction of children, youth, and adults according to the methods of modern pedagogy.

Gradually the theological foundations of the religious education movement began to crumble, and by the late 40s and 50s most mainline denominations had adopted, in varying degrees, the theology of neo-orthodoxy. Religious education changed its name to Christian education, but the image of the church school and religious instruction remained intact. Large educational plants modeled after modern public school architecture and equipped with the latest in educational technology were built wherever economically feasible. More professionals were hired by local churches to direct these burgeoning educational institutions attached to local churches, and denominational curriculum resources erupted as big business.

During the 60s a few significant voices spoke out for a broader understanding of Christian education—Randolph Crump Miller, D. Campbell Wyckoff, C. Ellis Nelson, Robert Havighurst, Roger Shinn, Ross Snyder, Rachael Hendrilite, and Sara Little, to name a few. They boldly attempted to make the case that effective programs of Christian education needed to be planned in the light of the total mission and ministry of the church. They acknowledged that the church teaches most significantly through nurture in a worshiping, witnessing community of faith, and they clearly explained that explicit instruction in the church schools was only a small part of Christian education. Nevertheless, even they placed special emphasis on the church school and on instruction; few heard their call for a broader perspective.

We now find ourselves in the 70s with the foundations of neo-orthodoxy eroded, and seemingly unable to envision any significant alternative to the church. Rachael Hendrilite reminds us that we can't go home again, C. Ellis Nelson emphasizes religious socialization, and Randolph Crump Miller shifts his attention to theological foundations. A few voices, like Edward A. Powers in his book, *Signs of Shalom,* repeat the earlier call for a broader understanding of Christian education and an attempt to provide a new theological foundation. Nevertheless, local church folk still ask for help in revitalizing their church schools without any particular theological foundation. A host of panaceas in the form of methodologies or new variations on the church school, such as family clusters, flourish for a time and denominations still strive to produce curriculum resources.

Vast amounts of money continue to be spent on teacher training, educational technology, and buildings. Numerous colleges have developed degree programs in Christian education to supply churches with economical semiprofessionals to save and revitalize their church schools. Denominations develop public relations campaigns to save the church school, and salvation by a new curriculum is still promised. A few reversals in past trends, or even a leveling off in the attendance decline, give people new hope, but still our educational ministries flounder. A broader perspective from which to evaluate, plan, and engage in Christian education is still not understood, or accepted. Some continue to offer a prophetic word and preach about alternatives, but little appears to change. Why?

THE PROBLEM

I am convinced that the very foundations upon which we engage in Christian education are shaking. And while a host of builders attempt with varying degrees of success to shore them up, there is a dearth of architects engaged in designing new structures. The church's educational problem rests not in its educational program, but in the paradigm or model which undergirds its educational ministry—the agreed-upon frame of reference which guides its educational efforts.

Every field of endeavor operates out of some common frame of reference or identity. Most often we take this orientation for granted; it guides our work, helps us shape our questions, and provides us with insights for solutions to our problems. The paradigm within which we labor tells us what to do and provides us with a language to share our efforts with others.

Religious educators hold in common certain assumptions about their endeavor. The language of religious education subject matter, what we want someone else to know—is an expression of those understandings. The set of assumptions, orientation, and frame of reference which informs us is expressed in the paradigm by which we engage in educational ministry. Since the turn of the century, in spite of nods to other possibilities, Christian educators and local churches have functioned according to a *schooling-instructional paradigm.* That is, our image of education has been founded upon some sort of a "school" as the context and some form of instruction as the means. Seminaries, denominational bureaucracies, educational professionals, and local church lay persons have all shared this common perspective.

Within the confines of this model, a great number of imaginative, important, and relevant contributions to Christian education have been made; and a significant influence on the lives of adults, youth and children can be observed. It is only natural, therefore, that we have assured ourselves that improving the techniques and resources of schooling and instruction will continue to solve our education needs. But, limited by a once helpful model, we have blindly and unconsciously proceeded as if there were no other possible way. Attempts to broaden that perspective, while intellectually acknowledged, are functionally resisted, and so we continue to let the schooling-instruction paradigm define our problem and establish the criteria for choosing questions to be addressed. As a result, particular issues are acknowledged and only certain questions answered. The schooling-instructional paradigm isolates us from new possibilities while continuing to occupy most of our attention in teaching, research, practice, and resource development. To compound our difficulties, we find it functionally difficult to imagine or create any significant educational program outside it.

Of course, this is not uniquely a problem of the church. The church mirrors the society in that education in the United States operates according to a similar paradigm. Any attempt to de-school society or question the adequacy of instruction is either ignored or met with hostility. The schooling-instructional paradigm has dominated our thinking for some time, but not always. Recall that Plato, in all his discussions of education, gives little attention to schools. As far as Plato was concerned, it is the community that educates, by which he meant the multiplicity of formal and informal forces which influence persons.

In this century, John Dewey began his important career by assuring us that all of life educates, and that instruction in schools represents only one small part of our total education. Furthermore, he insisted that there were many forms of deliberate education. At that point Dewey was a Platonist, but late in his life, confronted by urbanization and the technological revolution, he reflected on education in American society and contended that education in the home, church, and community was no longer adequate for the day. Supported by this conclusion, he made the great twentieth-century theory jump: the school must do it. From that moment on the education in the United States has been functionally coexistent with schooling and instruction. If persons are killed on the highways, we add driver education; if girls have children out of wedlock, we add sex education. No matter what the problem or need, we organize a course. Schooling and instruction have become the panaceas for all our needs. Of course our schooling and instructional methods are continually reformed, but our faith in them is never questioned.

The church, mirroring the culture, operates according to a similar paradigm, and for about the same reasons. Professional religious educators at the turn of the century didn't feel that the old school, with its dependence upon other related institutions— home, country, church, and public school—could do the job. Thus, they focused their attention on a reformed church school that could do the job by itself. Consequently, no matter what the church's needs, our typical solution has been to develop courses of instruction for the church's school.

I contend that we have become victimized by this schooling-instructional understanding of religious education and imprisoned by its implications. As long as it informs our labors, significant alternatives will have difficulty becoming born or sustained.

While admitting that learning takes place in many ways, church education has functionally equated the context of education with schooling and the means of education with formal instruction. The public schools have provided us with our model of education, and insights from secular pedagogy and psychology have been our guides. A church school with teachers, subject matter, curriculum resources, supplies, equipment, age-graded classes, classrooms, and, where possible, a professional church educator as administrator, has been the norm. All this must change.

ANOMALIES

While some paradigm is necessary if we are to engage in any significant endeavor, any particular frame of reference may limit our awareness of new possibilities and act as a barrier to alternative understandings. Unaware of the character and limitations of the paradigm which informs our efforts, we are in danger of missing the anomalies—irregularities or deviations—that question our frame of reference. Even as we operate according to some agreed-upon understanding, it is important to be aware of the anomalies that question its viability. Of course, anomalies are not easily spotted or acknowledged.

Jerome Bruner once carried out an experiment in which he took a deck of cards and flashed them on a screen at differing rates of speed. In that deck he had placed a red ace of spades and a black four of hearts and at first no one saw the unusual cards. Rather, they corrected them and reported a black four of spades and red ace of hearts. Some sensed that something was not right—that an anomaly was present—but even when Bruner flashed the cards slowly, one at a time, some persons couldn't spot any anomalies. In a similar way, assumptions can limit our awareness, and while assumptions help us to achieve a stable consensus, they are typically conservative and so make it difficult to alter our understanding and ways, even in the face of compelling evidence that we should do so.

This, I contend, is the problem we face in Christian education today. We have accepted the assumptions of the schooling-instructional paradigm and missed the anomalies which make it no longer viable for our educational mission and ministry.

THE SMALL CHURCH

Following the lead of the public school movement, religious educators focused their attention on church schools—new educational institutions. Soon these institutions were divorced from the people and from church life, and rarely were they able to meet the needs of any but our larger, sophisticated, suburban churches.

Recently, I discovered the large, important world of the small church. As a professional church educator, I had often ignored these thousands of small churches and, like other church educators, I had gotten used to talking about educational plants, supplies, equipment, curriculum, teacher training, age-graded classes, and learning centers with individualized instruction. Lately, I've been confronted by churches which share a pastor and will probably never be able to afford the services of a professional church educator. At best they have a couple of small inadequate rooms attached to their church building, no audiovisual equipment, few supplies, an inadequate number of prospective teachers, and not enough students for age-graded classes. The Sunday church schools in these small mainline Protestant churches are sick—in part because they have tried to become modern church schools and failed. The Sunday school "statistics board" in the front of their churches dramatizes their situation and denominational programs, most of which they are unable to use, and creates feelings of inadequacy and failure.

Depression results from the realization that the great majority of Protestant churches have less than two hundred members. Many of these churches have nevertheless faithfully striven to turn their Sunday schools into church schools and have failed. The severity of the problem is great. One anomaly, the schooling-instruction paradigm, can be seen in the realization that most small churches will never be able to mount up or support the sort of schooling and instruction upon which religious education has been founded since the turn of the century.

ETHNIC CHURCHES

Also consider the numerous ethnic churches in our country. At one time I was the liaison person for the United Church Board for Homeland Ministries with our churches in Hawaii, and on one of my visits I met with the members of a number of small native Hawaiian churches. They still called their church schools Sunday schools, although through the years they had obediently and faithfully striven to develop a Christian education program, like that recommended by the church's educational professionals. They struggled to raise money to build classrooms, they bought the denomination's curriculum resources, and they sent their people to teacher training workshops and lab schools. And yet attendance continued to drop, teachers were difficult to secure and, more seriously, the faith was not being adequately transmitted or sustained.

They asked me why they were failing, and I was stunned. They were doing everything we had suggested and still they were unsuccessful. In desperation, I asked them to tell me about the days when they were succeeding. They explained that a number of churches gathered each Sunday evening for a luau. Young and old came together to sing hymns, tell the Gospel story, witness to their faith, discuss their lives as Christians, minister to each other's needs, eat, and have fellowship. They did almost everything natural to their culture except dance, which we had taught them was "immoral." When they finished describing their old educational programs, I could think of nothing but to suggest they return to having luaus, knowing that those committed to schooling and instruction think me mad.

A BROKEN ECOLOGY

While most of our Protestant churches are small, some seventy percent of all church members reside in churches of three hundred or more people, and one might conjecture that the schooling-instruction paradigm is viable in these churches. During the last few years I have visited a number of large dynamic church schools directed by qualified, creative, professional staffs. And I have found that there are quite a few churches where the dream of "the perfect" church school has been actualized. In these churches, most of the teachers are well-trained and many have developed their own exemplary curriculum resources. The educational plants, equipment, supplies, and organization would make many a public school envious. Attendance at church school has not significantly diminished, and there is still enthusiasm for their many innovative programs. And yet, in almost every case they have evaluated their achievements and found them lacking. The modern church school at its very best is less than adequate for our day. The reason is another anomaly in the schooling instructional-paradigm.

During the first third of this century an "ecology"—a pattern of relations between organisms and their environment—of institutions was consciously engaged in religious education. First, there was the community. Life in any typical American town nurtured persons in a Protestant ethos and atmosphere. Others—Roman Catholics, Jews, and others—lived and were nurtured in their own homogeneous communities.

Second, the family was basically secure, extended, and stable. There was little mobility; both parents were frequently home and shared family life together. And if not living under the same roof, relatives lived nearby and were in continuous interaction with the family. Divorce was less frequent, few women worked outside the home, and families were larger. There were few one-parent families and almost no interfaith marriages. Most persons were nurtured, married, and died within a hundred miles of their birth. In this environment, the family provided a natural setting and made a significant contribution to a person's religious education.

Third, most public schools were Protestant parochial schools. From the daily morning ritual of Bible reading (King James Version) and the Lord's prayer (with a Protestant benediction) to the textbooks complete with moral and religious lessons (The McGuffey Readers), children acquired general foundational Protestant religious education. Roman Catholics, in turn, supported their own parochial school system to educate their children.

Fourth, there was the church. The typical church was a community neighborhood congregation where all ages knew each other and regularly interacted. Many hours were spent at the church, not only in worship but in a variety of social activities. Here persons were socialized in the shared understandings and ways of their particular denomination.

Fifth, a great number of popular religious periodicals provided the major source of "entertainment" and religious education in the home.

Sixth and last, the Sunday school completed this ecology of institutions deliberately engaged in religious education. (Roman Catholics depended on courses in religion taught by nuns in the parochial schools.) The Sunday school was especially important in that it was a lay-directed organization where women could play a significant leadership role. It provided an intergenerational setting where persons could celebrate Easter, Christmas, Thanksgiving, Missionary Day, and Dedication Day. Always concerned about community, celebration, the religious affections, and the biblical story, these Sunday schools included plays and musicals, games, hikes and hunts, homecomings and family gatherings, parties and picnics, social service projects and community activities.

These six institutions intentionally worked together to produce an effective educational ecology.

But now an anomaly is found in our changing situation, for today most communities (especially those in which we find our larger churches) are heterogeneous. A pluralism of religious and secular persuasions interact and compete, and no longer can the community be counted upon to transmit a particular set of under-standings and ways.

The family has changed also. Families are smaller and children often lack any significant direct interaction with the grandparents and relatives. Increasingly, both parents work outside the home, actual or functional one-parent families are on the increase, inter-faith marriages are common. And the average family moves fre-quently and is typically without roots. Many functions of the family once carried out in the home have been assumed by the society. Day-care centers for children, retirement homes for the aging, rec-reation organizations for youth, and hospitals for the care of the sick are but a few examples of these now transferred functions.

The public school is now the religiously neutral institution intended by the Constitution, where at best religion can be taught *about* and studied objectively. Fewer Roman Catholics now send their children to parochial schools.

Today the church is rarely the center of people's social and community life; it is not uncommon for families to go away on weekends and find their numerous needs met in a diversity of secular groups. Television and an array of mass secular media have replaced religious publications.

So we are left with a church school (or parish Confraternity of Christian Doctrine (C.C.D.) program) struggling to do alone what it took an ecology of six institutions to do in the past. It cannot be done, but the schooling-instructional paradigm ignores this changing situation.

THE HIDDEN CURRICULUM

For a variety of reasons, the schooling-instructional paradigm inadequately addresses the educational needs of both the small and large church. More important, however, is an anomaly in the schooling-instructional paradigm that affects them both; namely the manner in which this paradigm eliminates the processes of religious socialization from the concern and attention of church educators and parishioners.

By socialization I mean all those formal and informal influences through which persons acquire their understandings and ways of living. For example, I have friends who have one child. The mother is a professional journalist who travels a great deal, and the father has willingly performed most of the parenting functions for their young daughter. On one occasion I observed the little girl playing house. Noticing that she was holding a doll, I inquired, "Who are you?" "I'm the father," she explained. "Oh, where is the mother?" I asked. "Well, she's away writing a story." That is socialization. No one intentionally sat down and taught this young girl that fathers take care of children and mothers work; she learned it without a school or instruction.

Education correctly understood is not identical with schooling. It is an aspect of socialization involving all deliberate, systematic and sustained efforts to transmit or evolve knowledge, attitudes, values, behaviors, or sensibilities. The history of religious education, therefore, needs to include the family, public schools, community ethos, religious literature, and church life. Schooling, on the other hand, is only one specific and very limited form of education. The schooling-instructional paradigm has made this small part into the whole and, by accepting this understanding, we have typically forgotten that even in the school the "hidden curriculum" of socialization is at work influencing what is learned.

Recently, I have been engaged in the study of schools and sex-role stereotyping. While visiting an elementary school, the principal thought I should visit a class using a new unit on human sexuality. What amazed him was my greater interest in walking through the halls. He asked to join me in my walk, and we observed the following: female teachers go into both the boys' and girls' rooms while male teachers go into only the boys' room; girls and boys are encouraged to play very different sorts of games; teachers correct or punish boys and girls in significantly different ways; there are no male teachers in the kindergarten and no female administrators; photographs in classrooms consistently have men and women in sex-defined roles. Later we talked and I tried to explain that no intentional course of study could adequately counter the hidden curriculum of that school. Indeed, it was daily life in that school which primarily affected persons' understandings and ways.

The same can be said about the church and the church school, but the schooling-instructional paradigm tends to isolate the process of socialization from our consideration. Because the informal hidden curriculum in our churches is often more influential than the formal curriculum of our church schools, the schooling-instruction paradigm will always be less than inadequate for the evaluation and planning of Christian education. For example: Once I taught a senior high class in worship, in which we learned that the offering was a symbolic, communal act in response to the Gospel of the people's intentions and commitments for life in the world. The class decided that the church's offering of money once a year for racial justice did not meet the criteria of an offering, and they suggested asking the congregation to place on the altar an offering of signed fair housing pledge cards. After a few minutes of discussion at a board meeting, the church's adult leaders turned down the suggestion on political and economic grounds. Where was the more significant learning, in the church school class or at the board meeting?

We can teach about equality in our church schools, but if our language in worship excludes women, if positions of influence and importance are held only by men or those from upper socioeconomic classes, or if particular races are either implicitly or explicitly excluded from membership, a different lesson is learned. Naming rooms in churches after wealthy donors may only teach children that the Christian life is one of gaining affluence. If we organize the church so that whenever time or talents are requested it is for serving the institutional needs, people are not apt to learn that the Christian life is one of mission in the world. And so it goes. As long as we operate by schooling-instructional paradigm, numerous significant influences will be ignored.

THE WRONG QUESTIONS

We continue to accept the established as real; we assume that if we know more about teaching and learning, we can solve our educational problems. Faced by curricular needs, we turn to technology and neglect new ways of being together. Faced with nonresponsive students, we turn to psychology to understand and control behavior instead of reflecting on the meaning of two persons in relationship. Confronted by difficulties in classroom discussion, cooperation, or morale, we consider the latest group-dynamics technique instead of rethinking the nature of community. When facing new problems, we typically respond by focusing even more sharply on formal teaching and learning, believing that it is possible, with new knowledge and techniques, to build a workable school for the church, train an adequate number of capable teachers, and provide more useful curriculum resources for quality church education. In bondage to this inadequate understanding, we interpret any small success or reversal of existing negative trends in church schooling as a confirmation of the old paradigm's validity. This anomaly in the schooling-instructional paradigm, therefore, relates to the sources of influence which inform its life. We have permitted the behavioral sciences to give us a source of false optimism.

We have assumed that the more we know about people and learning, the more effective will be our educational efforts. We have believed that if stages of thinking can be identified, then both resources and teaching techniques to answer all our educational needs can be designed. However, our deepest problems may be of a different nature. Perhaps we need to rethink and reshape the institutions within which people dwell, and begin struggling with what it means to be Christian together.

Another example results from the unfortunate fact that the schooling-instructional paradigm encourages adults to be with children in ways that assert their power over them. The language of teaching, learning, behavioral objectives, and subject matter tend to produce a mind-set that results in the tendency to inflict on children adult ways of being in the world. It is difficult for us simply to be with the neophyte in song, worship, prayer, storytelling, service, reflection, and fellowship. We always seem to want to do something to or for them so they will be like us or like what we would like to be.

But education grounded in Christian faith cannot be a vehicle for control; it must encourage an equal sharing of life in community, a cooperative opportunity for reflection on the meaning and significance of life. Surely we must share our understandings and ways with children, but we also must remember that they have something to bring to us and that what we bring to children is always under God's judgment. Of course, it is easier to impose than reflect, easier to instruct than share, easier to act than to interact. It is important, however, to remember that to be with a child in Christian ways means self-control more than child-control.

To be Christian is to ask: What can I bring to another? Not: What do I want that person to know or be? It means being open to learn from another person (even a child) as well as to share one's understandings and ways. To speak of schooling and instruction leads us in other directions and to other conclusions. Should we not ask: Is schooling and instruction in a Christian community necessary for education? Or is living as a Christian with others inherently educational? If we attend to being Christian with others, need we attend to schooling and instruction? By focusing on schooling and instruction we have ignored these issues and questions that are so important for Christian faith.

RELIGION OR FAITH

We have too easily linked the ways of secular education with religion. Dependence upon the practice, rhetoric, and norms of secular psychology and pedagogy is risky business. Perhaps there is something unique about education in religious communities. That uniqueness is made clear in the last anomaly I wish to mention.

This anomaly surfaces in the awareness of what purposes schooling and instruction best serve. Recall the question asked in the Gospel according to St. Luke: "When the Son of Man comes will he find faith on earth?" (Luke 18:8). Surely he will find religion (institutions, creeds, documents, artifacts, and the like), but he may not find faith. Faith is deeply personal, dynamic, ultimate. Religion, however, is faith's expression. For example, religion is concerned about institutions (churches), documents, statements of belief (Bible and theology), and our convictions and moral codes. Religion is important, but not ultimately important. Educationally, religion is a means not an end; faith is the only end. Faith, therefore, and not religion, must become the concern of Christian education.

The anomaly of the schooling-instruction paradigm is found in its natural and primary concern with religion. You can teach about religion, but you cannot teach people faith. Thus, this paradigm places Christian education in the strange position of making secondary matters primary. Teaching people *about* Christianity is not very important. Religion at best is an expression of someone's faith which, under proper conditions, can lead others to faith. Bach wrote the "B Minor Mass" as an expression of his faith, and I have faith in part because I am moved to faith whenever I hear it. However, knowing all about the "B Minor Mass" is not to be confused with having faith; indeed, one can know all about it and not be Christian at all.

It appears that as Christian faith has diminished, the schooling-instructional paradigm has encouraged us to busy ourselves with teaching *about* Christian religion. As our personal commitment to Christ has lapsed, many church persons have turned for solace to teaching children what the Bible says, what happened in the history of the church, what we believe, and what is right and wrong. Sometimes, even when the school has succeeded, it has only produced educated atheists. For many today, Christian religion as taught in our church schools stands between them and God. The schooling-instructional paradigm easily leads us into thinking that we have done our jobs if we teach children all *about* Christianity.

There is a great difference between learning about the Bible and living as a disciple of Jesus Christ. We are not saved by our knowledge, or beliefs, or our worship in the church; just as we are not saved by our actions or our religion. We are saved by the anguish and love of God, and to live according to that truth is to have faith.

Faith cannot be taught by any method of instruction; we can only teach religion. We can know about religion, but we can only expand in faith, act in faith, live in faith. Faith can be inspired within a community of faith, but it cannot be given to one person by another. Faith is expressed, transformed, and made meaningful by persons sharing their faith in an historical, tradition-bearing community of faith. An emphasis on schooling and instruction makes it too easy to forget this truth. Indeed, the schooling-instructional paradigm works against our necessary primary concern for the faith of persons. It encourages us to teach about Christian religion by turning our attention to Christianity as expressed in documents, doctrines, history, and moral codes. No matter what the rhetoric of our purposes, the schooling-instructional paradigm, modeled after modern psychology and pedagogy, leads us to focus on religion rather than faith. If for no other reason than this, the schooling-instructional paradigm needs to be questioned.

A BANKRUPTCY

I have concluded, therefore, that the schooling-instructional paradigm is bankrupt. An alternative paradigm, not merely an alternative educational program, is needed. But that is easier said than done. Our dilemma is exemplified in a Sufi story about a person who, having looted a city, was trying to sell an exquisite rug. "Who will give me a hundred pieces of silver for this rug?" he cried. After the sale was completed, a comrade approached the seller and asked, "Why did you not ask more for that priceless rug?" "Is there a number larger than one hundred?" asked the seller.

Until we can imagine an alternative to our present schooling-instructional paradigm, our efforts at Christian education will be inadequate and increasingly ineffective. However, a new paradigm cannot be created in a vacuum. Christian education is dependent upon theological underpinnings, a fact that we have forgotten on occasion; relying, rather, upon insights from philosophy, the social sciences, or general education. Before we can explore an alternative paradigm, we must reflect on our theological convictions, so to that task we turn. But first a word of hope.

Unless hope is aroused and alive there is little reason to struggle with an alternative paradigm. Remember, therefore, that hope has its foundations in dissatisfactions with the present. Hope is founded upon the death of the old and the birth of the new. There are those who are troubled by death, the unknown, the new, but the Christian faith finds hope for tomorrow in the destruction of old ways and understandings.

Questioning our schooling-instructional paradigm provides us with a significant opportunity to rethink what we are about in religious education. It is not wise to depend on our own short, unreflective pasts or on our current endeavors to provide insight for the future, for when we do, we too easily accept the established as real. The future is in our imaginations and with God. In that conviction is our hope. As we celebrate the death of past understandings, we go forth, as pilgrims in faith, in search of new ones to support our educational ministry. We affirm the need to grapple with the radical question: Will our children have faith?

⚘

UPDATE

I continue to believe that the schooling-instructional paradigm is bankrupt, but I am less critical of the church school. I am more aware of the contribution it can make to a total education program. For example, it offers a body of knowledge such as the Scriptures as well as skills such as interpretation of Scriptures, making moral decisions, and thinking theologically. I am quite committed now to adult education in a schooling context. I am also more aware of the nurture that can take place with children in the church school. Nevertheless, a new paradigm is needed, and what I call a community of faith-formation paradigm is the one that best addresses the needs of our life. But more about that in the Afterword.

A rational faith requires the acquisition of knowledge and skills. In affirming the intuitive way of thinking and knowing, the pre-ration, I neglected the importance of the intellectual way of thinking and knowing. Christians do need to know the content of Scripture and how to interpret it; they need to have knowledge of ethical principles and to be able to make moral decisions; they need to know historic Christian doctrine and how to think theologically. I have found it helpful to understand how cognitive skills develop. First comes knowing — being able to repeat what I am told or read; second, comprehension — being able to put what I read or am told into my own words; third, application — making use of what I have learned in conversation and the sharing of ideas; fourth, analysis — understanding how another person thinks and has arrived at a particular position and being able to compare and contrast different positions; fifth, synthesis — being able to put together various positions and make my own considered opinion; and last, evaluation — being able to judge the value or worth of different positions. Since many adults have never learned to think about theological subjects, they argue about irrational opinions with passion, thereby dividing the church. Through instruction people can learn to discuss different conclusions in a rational manner and remain in communion with those with whom they differ.

I still believe that the most important exercise we can perform is asking new questions. Today I have more questions and fewer answers than I did in 1976. I am less critical and more open. I am less sure of myself and more questioning. I am less sure I know what to do, but more hopeful—hopeful because I am more sure that

God's spirit is present and active in human life and history. I am more confident that simple, faithful gestures are all that is required of us. To be faithful is to be present and patient wherever we find ourselves—that is, to neither run nor fight. To be faithful is to open ourselves spiritually to God and to discern what God is trying to do so that we might cooperate.

We have experienced only one other millennium change. The year 1000 was dark at best, and dire predictions of the world's end were common. Today as then, many sense our world's darkness, and apocalyptic prophesy is common. There are those who believe, now as then, that God has predestined to end human history in our time. They say that the signs of the times are clear and we must accept Jesus Christ as our savior before God brings down the final curtain on history. The issue is saving individual souls before it is too late.

At the same time there are others who are convinced that life has never been better and that we can create a new prosperous world through our human efforts. It is only a matter of time until we know enough to manage history, nature, and our society. Such people believe that there may be problems to be faced but the future is bright.

I find neither of these extremes useful. We are facing neither imminent destruction nor a new world. We face an age of significant and radical transformation, a time to critically reflect on our personal and social lives (the real purpose of transitional centuries and millennial times) and open ourselves to God so as to discern what God has in mind for us in this new era in God's history.

I have learned that most people either want to leave everything to God or to humanity. Those who believe that God is in charge sit back and give God advice, and eventually they lose faith that God can make a difference. Those who believe that we are in charge may ask God for advice and then act, but they too eventually lose faith that we humans can make a difference.

Both are unaware that God has created a world in which God can accomplish nothing without our help and we can accomplish nothing without God's help. For us the issue is to discern what God would like to accomplish and to ask God how we might cooperate, knowing that together all things are possible and there is hope.

CHAPTER TWO

Beginning and Ending with Faith

Religious educators must find a more dynamic theology for the emerging age or resign themselves to the inevitable eclipse of their movement in the American church.

H. Shelton Smith

A challenge confronts us, for not only do we face the crisis of a bankrupt paradigm, we face a corresponding crisis in our theological foundations. Inevitably, that places us in a particularly acute situation, for Christian education is dependent upon the theological underpinnings which judge and inspire its efforts. We would be foolish to attempt the description of an alternative paradigm without first exploring some theological issues.

Today this task is complicated by the variety of theological positions which vie for our attention: conservative, evangelical, liberal, new Reformation, charismatic, third-world, black, feminist, hermeneutical, process, and eschatological. Most serious is the theological agnosticism, confusion, and pluralism that exists in most local churches and which religious educators have tended to accept too easily. It is one thing for theologians to argue divergent positions within an agreed-upon historical understanding of Christian faith, but the local church cannot develop an adequate educational ministry when the pluralism with which it lives lacks agreement on theological essentials. Indeed, the church cannot proceed to develop an educational ministry without a clear, acknowledged theological foundation. A unity of theology and education is a necessity, not a luxury.

HISTORIC ROOTS

The first two decades of this century witnessed the emergence of religious education as a major movement in American mainline Protestantism, and interest in it eclipsed every other aspect of church life. Influenced by liberal modes of theological thought from the previous century, the social Gospel, and the progressive educational theories of John Dewey, religious education had a mind and soul. At no point in American Protestantism did the social interpretation of the Gospel root itself more strongly than in the religious education movement. George Albert Coe's book, *A Social Theory of Religious Education* (Arno Press, 1969) is a landmark in our history and a work of continuing significance.

A number of liberal theological presuppositions laid the foundations and gave vitality to the religious education movement. With regard to human nature, they emphasized a person's capacity for good. The significance of personal experience was affirmed. Sin was understood primarily as error or limitation, both of which could be addressed by education. A strong emphasis on moral education accompanied this liberal understanding of persons. Optimistic about the destiny of the human race, the kingdom of God was given a this-worldly interpretation. Convinced that with proper education persons could contribute to the building of God's kingdom within the natural historical process, the liberals emphasized the imminence of God and his social kingdom. Religion and ethics were made inseparable. Coupled with convictions of the social Gospel movement, religious education affirmed education's important role in the salvation of society.

However, history never remains fixed. Social situations change, and with them our theological positions. In the 30s a new theological voice was heard. Liberalism had reached its zenith and neo-orthodoxy was born as a necessary corrective to its extremes. Personal experience was now to be depreciated while the centrality of the Scriptures and the authority of the biblical revelation was announced. Sin was identified as more than human ignorance; it was the natural corruption of the will. Salvation could no longer be understood as a product of education, and the expectation that we humans could build the kingdom of God was dispelled. Instead, God's kingdom was understood as a judgment over all human achievements. Countering liberalism's belief in the social self, neo-orthodoxy affirmed the individuality of persons, each of whom lives under the judgment and grace of God. Conversion was once again emphasized as necessary for salvation, and the church was called to its uniqueness as a community of the saints set apart from the world.

The impact of neo-orthodoxy on the church's educational ministry was great. Religious education was transformed into Christian education. As a "Johnny-come-lately" to this theological reversal, I have always been troubled by the way in which the corresponding truths in liberalism and neo-orthodoxy became estranged. Christian education, I contend, paid a great price for the church's inability to reconcile and unite these two complementary (often paradoxical) theological positions.

From my readings of Scripture, liberal theology correctly affirmed God's indwelling presence and action in the world process. History is intentional and directional and God is perpetually and universally acting in the world of nature, persons, and society. Neo-orthodoxy, on the other hand, rightly reclaimed God's transcendence. God acts in history but is not to be identified with history. We do not fully comprehend who God is or how God works, but God does reveal himself in God's historical actions. Society and persons are fallen, and God acts over against his fallen creation to redeem it. Nevertheless, God also acts in and through the lives of persons and nations to do his will. Liberal theology emphasized the historical personage of Jesus, his human example and ethical importance, but ignored his divine nature as Jesus Christ and his importance as God's saving action in the world. Liberal theology correctly affirmed the importance of personal experience but neglected the authority of Scripture and tradition which both inspires and judges all personal experience. Liberalism rightly affirmed the social self and the social nature of the Gospel and salvation, while neo-orthodoxy rightly reminded us of the individual converted soul's importance.

A DECISION

Now once again we who are responsible for Christian education in the church are confronted with a crucial decision: What theological orientation will inform our labors? The religious education movement was an offspring of liberal theology, and when neo-theology emerged, its influence was felt. H. Shelton Smith, caught in the midst of this struggle between liberalism and neo-orthodoxy, correctly reminded the church in his important book, *Faith and*

Nurture, of the essential unity between education and theology. He also wisely sought to build a bridge between liberalism's concern for the social order and neo-orthodoxy's concern for the tradition. But at the time (1940s) there was no acceptable theology to hold these two positions together, and his message went unheard. Today, liberation theology makes possible a synthesis of these two historic theological movements. Moreover, liberation theology makes possible important coalitions between Roman Catholic and Protestant (witness the ecumenical character of its adherents); liberals and conservatives (witness the continuing concerns of the World Council of Churches and the new evangelical witness in the Chicago Declaration); majorities and minorities (witness the number of theological books written from a black, feminist, third-world, and Anglo-white perspective).

Therefore, while each of the numerous current theological positions vying for attention offers valuable insights, I contend that liberation theology provides the most helpful theological system for Christian education today. This conviction is founded upon my belief that liberation theology makes possible the long-avoided and essential unification of neo-orthodoxy's concern for the historic Christian tradition with liberalism's concern for justice and the social order. In the past our educational efforts have been informed by the one or the other, but now a new synthesis is possible. Liberation theologians—Herzog, Cone, Ruether, Gutierrez, Russell, Roberts, Alves, and others—may differ, but they all share common methods, perspectives, and themes. In terms of method, liberation theology understands theology as critical reflection on the activity of God in history. Theology is drawn from our human experience and our common search for the right questions as well as the right answers. This form of practical theology brings action and reflection together; it unites Scripture, tradition, and experience.

Liberation theology also shares three common perspectives on the experience of God in history. First is the biblical promise of liberation. God is the one who sets people free, and the Gospel announces the good news of liberation. God is biased toward the marginal people—the have-nots, the oppressed, the hurt, the outsiders. Christ has set and is setting the captives free. Second, life is understood as centered in history and is changing and changeable. That is, life is a series of events moving the world in the direction God intends. Liberation theology asserts that we have hope because we have a memory of God's past acts in history; and we have purpose because God has given us a vision of the future God intends. Third, salvation is a social event in the present, not an escape from history but an engagement within history.

Finally, the uniting theme of liberation theology is the humanization of persons and institutions. The continuing struggle of the faithful Christian is centered in the call to act accordingly. Liberation theology affirms that we are responsible for shaping history and that we can join God in God's history-making. Education as action/reflection can play a significant role in helping us to live, individually and corporately, under the judgment and inspiration of the Gospel to the end that God's will be done and God's community (kingdom) comes.

Within this general understanding of liberation theology, however, there are specific theological issues especially important for the church's educational mission and ministry which need to be addressed. What follows is not a theological system or a theology for Christian education, but rather reflections on a series of theological issues. Like most theological statements they will be incomplete and perhaps slanted, but every generation is called upon to reflect on its historic tradition and to interpret that tradition for its own day. To respond to that call is to decide what issues must be addressed and hence emphasized. I have chosen those which I believe are most crucial for the church's educational mission and ministry. They are: the nature of God, revelation, and authority; the nature of the persons, conversion, and nurture; the nature of the church, discipleship, and individual-social life. To these issues we turn now. My responses are not meant to be complete or definitive, but they are meant to provide a theological framework for religious education and foundations for the development of an alternative to the schooling-instructional paradigm.

GOD

(I am troubled as to how to speak of God. He/she seems right, but perhaps only the word *God* should be used. I do not want to distort the nature of God nor ignore the justice due those who are left out and estranged by masculine language. Forgive, therefore, my lack of imagination and read each "he" as intended; that is, as pointing to God, inclusive of all those characteristics culturally attributed to women and/or men— the creator, liberator, and comforter of all people.)

There is only one place a theology for education can begin— with God, the God who acts and thereby discloses himself and his intentions for creation. God, in the Christian faith, refers to the *one who acts*. Over and over again the Bible emphasizes the deeds that God has done. The God of the Christian faith is a living, dynamic *will,* with purposes for the world and the power to realize them. God's will is for justice, equity, whole community, and the well-being of all. God's purposes are shaped by love using power to overcome oppression. God is a mystery and yet God reveals himself—his will, purposes, and power—in historic activity.

God is an agent. God acts in history on behalf of his coming community where justice, liberation, wholeness of life, unity, peace, and the well-being of all peoples are realized. That is the central affirmation to be made about God. It is the good news of what God has done in Jesus Christ.

The centrality of the Bible for Christian faith is derived from its record of God's activity. The Old and the New Testaments are important because they contain the story of God's actions in history and his people's attempt to understand and respond. From the biblical story, we also learn who we are and how we are to live. The historic interpretations and pronouncements of the church provide us with a continuing resource for understanding the story. Our individual and corporate experiences with God and others in history provide us with the context in which the story assumes meaning in each generation. The Bible, however, remains the source and norm of Christian faith.

Nevertheless, the written words of the Bible are not our final authority, nor are the doctrines of the church, nor are our own personal inner experiential convictions. While each provides us with one aspect of the authority upon which Christian faith is founded, it is God's historical liberating action in Jesus Christ that is the final authority and the foundation for Christian faith. In the life, death, and resurrection of Jesus Christ, God provides us with the basis for understanding, interpreting, and applying our faith story.

At the heart of our Christian faith is a story. And at the heart of Christian education must be this same story. When we evaluate our corporate lives as a community of faith, this story must judge us. Our ritual life, the experiences we have in community, and the acts we perform in the world must be informed by this story. Unless the story is known, understood, owned, and lived, we and our children will not have Christian faith. The struggle to know, understand, interpret, live, and do God's word must be at the center of our educational mission. For too long the church in its educational ministry has supported a strange and deafening silence. We have tried to live as if the story were unimportant. Only when the Christian story of God's actions in history becomes the focus of our educational ministry will that ministry be Christian. The Bible must once again become our one and only "textbook," for in its story we come to know the actor God who creates, redeems, and sustains life in the past, present, and future. Further, when the faith community's story becomes our story, God's presence among us as historic actor becomes a part of our experience.

PERSONS

We began with God because our understanding of God is prior and because every statement about God is finally a statement about persons. We are created by God in God's image. The best way to understand ourselves, therefore, is as historical actors. The human self, like God, is an *agent*. We act through the integration of our thinking, feeling, and willing, but the self is ultimately a doer. All meaningful knowledge is for action, and our knowledge is for action, and our knowledge of the world is a result of our actions in the world. We know God through God's actions and through participation with God in his actions; we know others through their actions and our interactions with them; we know ourselves through our actions and interactions with others.

We are historical actors, free and determined. We live a paradoxical existence in which we shape and are shaped, influence and are influenced. The world and the historical process is the meeting place of actors.

The self as actor is not an isolated individual. Our existence is dependent upon interactions with God and other persons. The isolated individual self is a fiction, but so is the social self. To affirm only a social self is to overemphasize the role nurture and socialization play in framing us. To affirm only the individual self, naked and responsible before God, is to underestimate the significance of other historical actors in our lives. In truth we are corporate selves who live in a continual dynamic relationship with all others and with God. The self is constituted by its relationships; human life is essentially corporate. God created human beings with a need for community, and therefore we cannot be human or Christian alone. Community and corporate identity are not optional. We are corporate selves who have been created to relate with God and each other—with all others—in freedom and responsibility. We may misuse our freedom and deny our responsibility by trying to live unto ourselves without God and others, or against God and others, yet we are still bound together. If any one person is oppressed, hurt, denied equity and justice, or kept marginal, we are all prevented from achieving full humanness.

Our created corporate selfhood places us in an essential relationship with *all* others. Because God is in relationship with all persons, we cannot be in full community with God unless we also identify with and seek the good of *all* persons. To reach this goal it is especially important for us to be biased (as God is biased) toward the oppressed and hurt, those outside the benefit of the system—that is, toward the have-nots of this world. Our human sin is revealed in both our denial of corporate selfhood (a denial which estranges us from God, neighbor, and self) and in our apathy and sloth (a condition which results from either believing we are not called to be responsible actors in the world or believing that we are only victims of history's determining forces).

Our human sin is revealed in our willingness to withdraw from the struggle of life, and our unwillingness to accept responsibility for history. As a result we become estranged victims of history, but God in his unmerited love acted in Christ to free us for responsible history-making. No longer need we be enslaved to those powers and institutions and practices which control and ultimately work to destroy us. We are liberated in Christ for historical action consistent with the will and purposes of God. Because of God's gracious act in the crucifixion and resurrection of Jesus Christ we have the power to join God in God's history-making, and thereby to be united with God, our neighbor, and ourselves. We are saved from the corruption of our image by an action of God alone and not by education. The Christian faith is not founded upon a Gospel of good works or advanced learning, but on the good news of God's action in Jesus Christ. Christian salvation is more than enlightenment or a scheme for good living. Salvation is God-given and not something we humans achieve by moralistic or pedagogical means. At the same time salvation is not solely an individual piety related only to personal relations with God and neighbor. The Gospel is a social Gospel, a worldly Gospel, or no Gospel at all.

Individually and corporately, we need to be converted to true freedom—freedom to act with God in history on behalf of liberation, justice, peace, unity, wholeness, community, and the well-being of all peoples.

In the not-too-distant past the church placed an emphasis on growth and social change through a gradual evolutionary process. Optimistic about the improvement of the race and social progress, we placed our emphasis on nurture. We neglected human nature and the need for radical change in our lives. The Gospel's call is to repentance. Human existence is in contradiction to God's community. We cannot do God's will through our own doing, nor can we build God's coming community. God will bring in God's community in God's good time, but God also calls us to join him in his community building.

Historically, Christian education has vacillated between a concern for conversion and a concern for nurture. With the birth of the religious education movement, nurture through teaching became the dominant underlying purpose. The acquisition of faith was understood in terms of nurture and growth which functionally correspond to a gradual process of schooling. Support for this position was located in a single phrase in Horace Bushnell's *Christian Nurture* (Yale University Press, 1966). A child is to grow up as a Christian and never know himself or herself as being otherwise. This dictum may have made sense when it referred to the children of the saints, who were to be nurtured in a church whose membership was restricted to the saints and their offspring. But I contend that the church can no longer surrender to the illusion that child nurture, in and of itself, can or will rekindle the fire of Christian faith in persons or in the church.

We have expected too much of nurture, for at is very best, nurture makes possible institutional incorporation. We can nurture persons into institutional religion, but not into mature Christian faith. The Christian faith by its very nature demands conversion. We cannot gradually educate persons through instruction in schools to be Christian. Of course, persons need to be and can be nurtured into a community's faith and life. There is a basic need to belong to and identify with a faithful community, to own its story as our story, and to have our religious affections nourished.

But persons also need, if they are to grow in faith, to be aided and encouraged to judge, inquire, question, and even to doubt that faith; to be given the opportunity to experiment with and reflect upon alternatives; and to learn what it means to commit their lives to causes and persons. Only after an intellectual struggle with our community's faith and with an honest consideration of alternatives can a person truly say "I believe,"—and thereby achieve personal Christian identity. Only then, I contend, can a person live the radical, political, economic, social life of the Christian in the world.

Conversion, I believe, is best understood as this radical turning from "faith given" (through nurture) to "faith owned." Conversion is radical because it implies ownership and the corresponding transformation of our lives. It implies a reorientation in our thinking, feeling, and willing; a moving from indifference or one form of piety to another. That is why conversion historically is only rarely a singular emotional outburst, a once-and-for-all dramatic occasion which can be dated and described. Rather, conversion is more typically a process by which persons are nurtured in a community's faith (the religion of the heart), go through the despair of doubt and the intellectual quest for understanding (the religion of the head), and at last, in late adolescence or early adulthood, experience illumination, certainty, and identity. In retrospect, most persons who achieve this mature conversion identify their early faith as inadequate and their earlier experiences of emotional conversion into the community's beliefs, attitudes, and values as insignificant.

Conversion, however, is never an isolated event devoid of all elements of nurture. Nurture and conversion are a unified whole. Neither those who nurture persons into church membership nor those who nurture persons into the acceptance of the church's dogma have taken seriously the relationship between nurture and conversion.

An example may help to explain my understanding of conversion as a reorientation of the soul, a deliberate turning from indifference or an earlier form of piety to passionate commitment to a new way of life. The life I would like to examine is that of Horace Bushnell, partly because he seems to have wanted to replace conversion with nurture, and partly because his experience is typical of almost every religious leader and saint in the history of the church. Bushnell was nurtured by religious parents in a nineteenth-century New England Congregational church. At seventeen, during a revival, he experienced a deep flow of religious feeling—"the Lord in his tender mercy led me to Jesus and saved my soul." At twenty-one he entered Yale College where his earlier religious fervor dulled and his skepticism grew. His mother hoped that he would prepare for the ministry, but Bushnell left Yale and went from teaching to journalism to law—all the time struggling with his doubts and trying to intellectualize his faith.

A few years later he returned to Yale as a tutor, only to find his pupils awaiting his words on faith. His inability to speak on the subject tormented him. He realized that he had substituted thought for everything else and, through his attempts to create a religion of the head, had pushed faith away. In prayer, he confessed to God his despair and his willingness to trust. The result was the clearing of doubt, a new enlightenment or illumination, and a commitment to enter the ministry. This later experience Bushnell describes as his true conversion to Christian faith, thereby discrediting his earlier conversion and the significance of his earlier religious experience.

Neither the pietist who has no commitment to the struggle for justice and righteousness in the world of institutional life, nor the social activist who has no personal commitment to Christ, is truly converted into mature Christian faith. True conversion—authentic Christian life—is personal and social life lived on behalf of God's will in the political, social, and economic world. The converted life is a revolutionary existence over against the status quo, a life committed to a vision of God's coming community of liberation, justice, peace, whole community, and the well-being of all people. We cannot be nurtured into such life—not in this world. Every culture strives to socialize persons to live in harmony with life as it is. The culture calls upon its religious institutions to bless the status quo and its religious educational institutions to nurture persons into an acceptance of it.

God calls his people to be signs of Shalom, the vanguard of God's coming community, a community of cultural change. To reach the conviction that such countercultural life is our Christian vocation, and to be enabled to live such a corporate existence in but not of the world, necessitates conversion as well as nurture.

Once again we need to understand that both conversion and nurture have a place in religious education if such education is to be Christian. Our sole concern for nurture has contributed to our losing both an evangelical power and a social dynamic. While rejecting a sterile revivalism, we constructed a false evangelism through nurture. Christian education for conversion means helping persons to see that they are called, not only to believe the church's affirmation that Jesus is the Christ but to commit their lives to live as his apostles and disciples in the world.

Persons, as corporate selves and historical actors, are in need of both nurture and conversion. The church's educational ministry must be founded upon this awareness.

CHURCH AND SOCIETY

One Christian is no Christian, for we cannot be Christian alone—we are created for community.

The church is best understood as a creation of God, a community of corporate social agents called to bear witness individually and corporately in word and deed to God's intention for human life, that is, to be a radical community for others, a countercultural community biased toward and acting with God on behalf of the oppressed, the hurt, the poor, the have-nots, the marginal people of the world.

The church can never exist for itself; it is never an end, only a means. Its mission, its end, is to be a community where Christian faith is proclaimed, experienced, understood, lived, and acted upon in history. But the church, while a saved community which bears the message of salvation, is also a fallen institution which often lives for itself.

A few months ago a group of my students and I engaged in a research project on rites of initiation in Protestant religious communities. Through the anthropological method of participant-observation we studied a large number of diverse groups. When we completed our work, we were forced to create a typology for rites of initiation: namely, rites of institutional incorporation and rites of faith commitment. In spite of the rhetoric of all groups that faith was their goal, we discovered that most mainline Protestant churches were primarily concerned with institutional incorporation and survival.

For example, confirmation classes were typically called membership classes, preparation centered on denominational polity, history, practice, financial support, participation in congregational life, and attendance at worship. The ritual itself had two sorts of questions. The first dealt with questions concerning faith and the second with institutional commitment. In every case we discovered that the leader of the ritual behaved in preferential ways toward the latter. One set of field notes after another disclosed that the faith questions were asked quickly, and answered in a similar manner. The minister then paused, looked the candidates in the eyes, spoke very slowly and listened very carefully for their reply to the questions on institutional loyalty. Is there any doubt which questions were considered more important? Also, when adults and parents were asked if they would be upset if their children decided not to be confirmed or baptized they typically said yes. But when asked why, they all replied that they would be lost as church members. No one expressed concern for their children's souls or faith.

Institutionally we may be less than Christian; still we are created by God for life in community. Our understanding of the Christian faith can never be individualistic. Christian life is to be lived in and for the community of God. Too often we have led persons to a life of mere inwardness or personal piety, thus blessing the existing social, political, and economic order regardless of the injustices they may perpetuate. The covenant of God's people with the Lord of history entails responsibility for the total character of society. Any restriction of religion to the immediate relation between an individual and God is a denial of the Christian story, which calls for the transformation of the whole of life. To believe that institutions will take care of themselves if individuals have personal faith is folly.

It is difficult to be or become a Christian when everyone claims the name. The Christian faith necessitates a converted radical community of faith within which to live and grow; a servant community which seeks the good of others, acts for the liberation of all

persons, and aids us all to resist private gain in the search for corporate selfhood.

We are *not* called to be incorporated into the church as one
institution among others. God intends that the church be a *unique*
witnessing community of faith, a converted, pilgrim people living
under the judgment and inspiration of the Gospel to the end that
God's will is done and God's community comes. The church is
called to be a community of corporate selves interacting with each
other and the world as an expression of their commitment to the
Lord of history.

We have sometimes neglected the church as God's chosen
people, a community of radical Christian faith, a prophetic community distinct from the world. But only such an understanding can
guide the church's life and mission.

Today, as in every age, the church struggles to be faithful to
God in the political, social, and economic world. We must not
equate Christian faith with any nation's way of life or with opposi-
tion to the ideologies of other nations. Nor can we afford to equate
Christian faith with any economic or social system. Instead we
must sense God's judgment on all political, social, and economic
systems, including our own.

Still God does not call us out of the world; he rather sends us
into the world. We therefore live as Christians when we discern
what God is doing in the world and join God in his work. Worship
should inspire and motivate us for such radical action.

Of course we will always risk disagreement and error when we
try to say what God is doing and what we must do, but the church is
called to live in that tension. To accomplish its mission the church
is required to live in the world but not of it. That is not easy to do,
of course. Every society asks of its religious institutions that they
bless the way things are, and that is why those churches which support the status quo are often the most popular. Though they deny

the Gospel, they fulfill the world's demand that they be communities of cultural continuity.

Christ calls his church, however, to be a community of change, to act with God in transforming the world into the community of our Lord and Savior Jesus Christ. To make an adequate response to that vocation is to live simultaneously in this world and in the community of God. We cannot escape from the world and be faithful. Neither can we become so enmeshed in the world that we lose our souls. To live on the boundary is difficult and demanding.

Nevertheless, the Scriptures remind us that we are a special people, a people with a peculiar memory—a memory of being continuously called to leave where we are and go somewhere else and be someone else, a people never staying put or holding on to present understandings and ways.

We are a people with a peculiar vision—a vision of a world not yet realized and yet already come. In our worst moments we stop envisioning and believe it is well to celebrate and keep life as it is, but God haunts us by promising us a new age and pulling us toward its realization. Continuously, God demands that we be dissatisfied with life as it is. God judges us and provides us with a vision to inspire and stimulate us to action.

We are called to be a people with a peculiar hope—a hope that gives meaning to life as a pilgrim people on a mission under the power and purpose of the Gospel. It is a hope which proclaims that persons and institutions can change, that people and the public order can be transformed to more fully embody God's will for justice, harmony, liberation, community, and peace.

But what counts for us humans is not realizing this hope, but resisting evil. What matters is the human struggle against all that denies God's coming community and to that end we are called.

In our most recent memories there have been two quite different responses to God's call to Christian responsibility. The first was the liberal progressivism of the social Gospel, with its commitment to the gradual human transformation of society through human action. Following a disillusionment over the assumption of inevitable progress and human goodness came neo-orthodoxy with its focus on human sin and a shift from political and social change to an emphasis on the redemptive acts of God in history, on judgment and realism. Each possessed partial truth. Each was a corrective for the other. Neither alone was adequate. Both have been caricatured and criticized by advocates of the other and by those who shared neither of their understandings of the social dimensions of the Gospel.

What is needed today is a new understanding that has no blind expectations of progress or belief in the capacity of human beings to build God's community. Founded upon a more radical understanding of God's action in history and a renewed social consciousness consistent with the biblical narrative, we need to work toward the equipping of persons and groups to engage in responsible action in society.

Along with the Christian faith through the ages we need to affirm that God is at work, especially in events and moments that liberate people from oppression and advance justice, peace, community, and well-being. God continues to reach out to those who suffer injustice, those who are excluded. Therefore, we believe that God sends us to work with others on behalf of God's coming community. We are charged to root out racism and prejudice from individuals and institutions, to correct the disparity between rich and poor nations, to stand with women and men of all races, ages, classes, and nationalities as they struggle for dignity, respect, power, and equity.

We know our efforts cannot bring in God's community, but faith plunges us into our struggle, and hope gives us courage and energy to live from reform to reform. God's new world and new humanity are surely coming, and we are called to live intelligently for that vision. Christian education must transmit this faith and hope. It must equip and stimulate us as individuals and churches to live for such ends. Only then can it truly claim the name Christian.

Ultimately the church exists for no other reason than to help make and keep human life genuinely human. That means that the church is to be that historic agency through which God overcomes the bondage to the institutions, power, and practices which have enslaved and oppressed persons and groups, enabling all persons to become the liberated, creative, visionary, historical actors as originally intended. It is, then, as a *witnessing community* that the church must be understood. The church has a story to tell, a vision to share, good news to proclaim. And that story, vision, and good news are communicated best through its life, its word-actions in the world. The structures and programs of the church can only be justified insofar as they enable the community of faith to be an historical agency through which God remakes the human world.

The church cannot afford to be an institution among institutions. It has a right to exist only as a body of disciplined believers committed to the historical mission of witnessing in word and deed to God's community-building.

The Christian church has no alternative but to engage in actions which challenge the evils of society—poverty, ignorance, disease, oppression, injustice, war, and prejudice—and to attempt to create more human alternatives. The Christian faith community therefore is called: to stop contributing to our social ills; to take a stand on social issues; to raise a prophetic voice against injustice; to take positive action on behalf of liberation; to influence public opinion; to join with others working for social justice; to identify with and become the advocate to the cause of the outsider; to eliminate the chasm between personal and social religion (why don't we turn the current enthusiasm for the Holy Spirit—long overdue— into a concern for the manifestation of the works of the Holy Spirit?); and to respond to people's hunger for spiritual life by relating worship and prayer to social action, for both together are the work (liturgy) of a faith community.

Some will say this is expecting too much of the church. But is that the issue? Perhaps the church has erred when it tried to make itself into a "perfect" community of "saints," but so did it err when it refused to set standards for its life and its members' lives. There is another possible position. The Christian community of faith can be clear on what it believes and what it is to be. Then, without ruling some people in and some out, or believing that it is always living the "perfect" life to which it is called, it can struggle continuously to live under the judgment and inspiration of the Gospel to the end that God's community comes and God's will is done. Only an educational paradigm that supports and encourages such an understanding of the church can be defended or advocated.

IMPLICATIONS

As a result of these theological musings, a few principles emerge that suggest directions for framing a new paradigm or model for religious education.

First, while maintaining a necessary particularity for education—deliberate, systematic, and sustained efforts—our new paradigm must broaden the context of Christian education to include every aspect of our individual and corporate lives within an intentional, covenanting, pilgrim, radical, counter-cultural, tradition-bearing faith community. A viable paradigm or model for religious education needs to focus upon the radical nature of a Christian community where the tradition is faithfully transmitted through ritual and life, where persons as actors—thinking, feeling, willing, corporate selves—are nurtured and converted to radical faith, and where they are prepared and motivated for individual and corporate action in society on behalf of God's coming community.

Second, while the context or place of Christian education is best understood as a community of faith, the means of Christian education is best understood as the actions between and among faithful persons in an environment that supports the expansion of faith and equips persons for radical life in the world as followers of Jesus Christ.

Therefore, *a community of faith-enculturation paradigm* is the name I have chosen for a new understanding of religious education. That may not be catchy or provide crystal-clear images, but it does suggest a direction for the future worth exploring, and it is to that task we turn next.

⚜

UPDATE

Constructive or systematic theology is always changing because its purpose is to make sense of the Gospel in a particular time and place. Liberation theology, which I raised up in this chapter, while still playing a role in my theology, is no longer dominant. I have added a host of contemporary attempts to understand the Gospel and its relevance for our lives including feminist theology. My present position, therefore, is more eclectic and broad.

I have become more aware of the wisdom in the Anglican principle of the *via media,* a theological conviction that truth is comprised of two opposite truths held in tension. For example, Jesus is fully human and fully divine. A heresy is a truth that neglects or denies its opposite. So many theological arguments and estrangements result from the inability or unwillingness of either side to acknowledge the truth in the other's position.

Recall that in the sixteenth century it appeared as if the Roman Catholic Church was teaching that there was a great deal people needed to do after they were baptized to achieve salvation. The Protestant Reformation seemed to maintain that salvation was given fully and completely at baptism and there was nothing anyone needed to do. Anglican theology attempted to take the position that defended the truth in both these positions. Baptism makes you aware of God's gift of salvation. It tells you the truth about your life. But then you spend the rest of your life becoming who you already are. That is, you need to live into your baptism. To put it another way, baptism makes known your justification through God's grace. Whole sanctification is something you participate in, with God's help, throughout your life.

One of my continuing concerns is not being clear on what we desire to achieve through our catechetical (educational) efforts. Our aim, I suggest, is to form Christ-like communal persons and communities. This implies for me clarity *of faith,* of how we are to perceive God. Many people have unhealthy images of God that need to be healed. Such images need to be healed until a God of unconditional, unmerited, never-ending love, a God whose justice is reconciliation, is the God with whom they seek a relationship. This is important because our images of God influence our moral behavior. Those who have an image of a vengeful God, for instance, are apt to support war and capital punishment as a means to achieve justice.

Faith is also concerned with how we perceive human beings and their lives. Many people have been raised with unhealthy perceptions of themselves. They have not learned what it means to reject the false self our culture would have us affirm and to love the self God loves, that is, the self that is in the image and likeness of God. To be in the image of God is to have breathed within us that divine spirit that seeks to be united with God and thereby experience holiness, wholeness, and health. To be in the likeness of God is to be a free agent who can know and do the will of God and thereby experience fullness and completeness of life. We have lost an understanding of our one common vocation: to grow into an everloving relationship with God and thereby with our true selves, all other

persons, and God's creation. We have neglected our one common
ministry, to love and serve, that is, to cooperate with God in every
moment and in every aspect of our life.

I cannot conceive of an individual human being. We are all persons in community. One Christian is no Christian. We are persons
in relationship with God and others, a totally dependent relationship
with God and an interdependent relationship with others. While we
cannot determine how another person lives, we all influence each
other. There is no way we can say for sure if our children will or
will not have faith, but of one thing we can be sure, they will never
have faith unless there is a community of faith for them to live in
and be influenced by. The community's faith always comes before
our own.

We humans have a soul, a unified body-mind-spirit. As such we
interact with our environment and all the various relationships that
comprise that environment (home, school, church, neighborhood,
media, etc.), we interact with our own genes, we interact with the
influence of evil in and about us, and we interact with God who
is also in and about us. We are never the victims of any of these
influences. We each choose which will play a dominant role in
our lives. We are truly free only when we choose the influence of
God. Because of this we must not have expectations or make claims
about the church's ability to form Christians. What is required are
intentional attempts to influence faithfully.

Another of my continuing concerns is *character*—a person's
sense of identity and how he or she is therefore predisposed to
behave. From my perspective, a Christ-like character is best summarized in the Beatitudes:

1. We are to be a people who know that we cannot manage
    history or nature, our political, social, and economic systems,
    or our own lives, and who live dependent upon God, trusting
    in God's grace and love.

2. We are to be a people who live self-critical lives, whose hearts are broken by the world's broken relationships and our own sin, who, having experienced God's reconciling love, recognize that our striving for reconciliation is never futile if we are willing to cooperate with God.

3. We are a people who neither love nor believe in ourselves too much or too little, but live humbly, abiding in God's reign, proclaiming by word and example (in all we say and do) the good news of God in Christ, by testifying to the possibility of knowing and doing God's will.

4. We are a people who have accepted the gift of God's unmerited, unending love and whose greatest desire is to live in an ever-deepening and loving relationship with God.

5. We are a people who are united with God in seeking and serving Christ in all persons through lives of compassion and forgiveness, loving all others as God loves us.

6. We are a people whose devotion to God runs so deep that we are disposed to know and do God's will with motives as pure and holy as our actions.

7. We are a people who have experienced God's justice as reconciliation and strive to restore all persons to a right relationship with God, themselves, all people, and the natural world.

8. We are a people who have integrity and who are willing to risk everything no matter what the price, including, if necessary, our lives, to be faithful to God's will.

And my final concern is *consciousness*—that subjective awareness that makes particular experiences possible, such as the presence and action of God in our lives, and the ability to discern God's will.

It is our commitment to such ends (faith, character, and consciousness) that needs to influence how we engage in our catechetical ministry.

CHAPTER THREE

In Search of Community

Faith is communicated by a community of believers and the meaning of faith is developed by its members out of their history, by their interaction with each other, and in relation to the events that take place in their lives.

C. *Ellis Nelson*

My contention is that the context or place of religious education needs to be changed from an emphasis on schooling to a community of faith. No longer is it helpful or wise to emphasize schools, teachers, pupils, curricula, classrooms, equipment, and supplies. Instead we need to focus our attention on the radical nature and character of the church as a faith community.

Ultimately, of course, a faith community is a gift from God, a mystery which we celebrate in the sacraments and acknowledge through lives lived under the judgment and inspiration of the Gospel. Nevertheless, a community of faith does seem to have certain characteristics that are identifiable and that can be helpful in evaluating our lives as a faithful people of God.

THE NATURE OF COMMUNITY

In a significant community the people share a common memory or tradition, common understandings and ways of life, and common goals and purposes. If such a community is to exist, there needs to be unity in essentials; that is, in the community's understandings, values, and ways. Diversity with a corresponding charity can only be tolerated in nonessentials, such as commitments to particular political, economic, or social causes, or to particular actions or strategies for change. A community possesses a clear identity. Pluralism is only possible or healthy when persons have an identity and are open to others. A faith community must agree on what it believes. Only then can the struggle to interpret those beliefs serve constructive ends. Diversity in interpretation can be valuable, but only if there is agreement on a statement of faith and the authority to be used as a guide to interpretation. Often the church tolerates too great a diversity in essentials and hence has no clear identity. When that occurs faith can neither be sustained nor transmitted, and community dissolves into institutional togetherness. Faith can only be nurtured within the self-conscious intentional community of faith.

Second, a community of faith must be small enough to maintain meaningful, purposeful interactions among its members. A church of over three hundred members can too easily avoid those interactions essential to the maintenance, transmission, and expansion of faith. Of course, in one important sense, the community of faith is universal, uniting together faithful persons of all tongues and races, here and beyond. However, for this greater community to have reality and meaning, we need to interact within the intimacy of a closely knit community in which fellowship and care for each other can be experienced, and in which the struggles of faith and life can be shared. Larger units can serve important organizational needs, but if they are to be fully constructive, we need to maintain the life of smaller communities within them. Without this sense of intimate community, the church becomes simply another institution in the society—and that we cannot afford to permit.

Third, true community necessitates the presence and interaction of three generations. Too often the church either lacks the third generation or sets the generations apart. Remember that the third generation is the generation of memory, and without its presence the other two generations are locked into the existential present. While the first generation is potentially the generation of vision, it is not possible to have visions without a memory, and memory is supplied by the third generation. The second generation is the generation of the present. When it is combined with the generations of memory and vision, it functions to confront the community with reality, but left to itself and the present, life becomes intolerable and meaningless. Without interaction between and among the generations, each making its own unique contribution, Christian community is difficult to maintain.

Last, a true community unites all those roles, and its understanding of status is important to corporate life. For the Christian this means that a true faith community must be composed of persons with diverse gifts—apostles, prophets, teachers. Yet how often has the church been willing to support prophets in its midst? However, when we avoid the pain and torment of a prophet's presence, a community of Christian faith eludes us. Also, when the Christian church is divided by race, social, or economic status, nationality or ethnic origin, true Christian community is once again outside our grasp. And of course, if one sex is restricted to particular roles or denied equal status, there can be no Christian community.

If our children are to have faith, we need to make sure that the church becomes a significant community of faith. To meet this challenge we need to take seriously the characteristic of community and we need to examine, evaluate, plan, and develop educational programs around three aspects of corporate life: the rituals of the people; the experiences persons have within the community; and the actions members of the community perform, individually and corporately, in the world.

RITUAL

By their rites will you know them is more that mere rhetoric, for no aspect of corporate life is more important than its rituals. Worship, therefore, is at the center of the church's life; indeed, the word orthodoxy means "right praise"—as well as "right belief." Ritual or cultic life sustains and transmits the community's understandings and ways. Our liturgies express the hidden meanings of our experience in relationship to the world, to others, and to God.

There is no community without cultic life. We humans are made for ritual and, in turn, our rituals make us. That is why our liturgies are so difficult to change. It will always be easier and more acceptable to preach a radical sermon than to change the order of worship, because the structures of our rituals provide us with the means to order and reorder life amidst the demands of daily existence and the vicissitudes of change. Rituals telescope our understandings and ways, give meaning to our lives, and provide us with purposes and goals for living. That explains why, when our understanding or ways of life change, we tend to stop participating in the old rituals that once inspired and sustained us. It also explains why, after casting aside old rituals, one of our first needs is to birth new ones. Changes in our understandings and ways result in changes in our rituals, and changes in our rituals produce significant changes in our lives. Every reform movement in the history of the church has involved liturgical reform; indeed, the most revolutionary events in Christian history have already affected the church's rituals. When the prophets sensed that the people had forsaken their faith, they attacked their rituals; and when people were in despair over their faith, they called them to return to their rituals.

Liturgy needs to become a major aspect of Christian education, but before that will be possible the character and role of rites and rituals need to be properly understood. Rituals are first of all orderly, predictable, and stereotyped. In a day when some old rituals have lost their meaning and we are experimenting with new rituals, we often forget the importance of order and predictability, which explains in part why those who are secure in past understandings are troubled by these experiments. Only those who are searching for new understandings find experiments with worship meaningful, but even they long for a day when order is reestablished. The church's educational ministry needs to assume responsibilities for helping the faith community to understand its ritual life, evaluate its present liturgies, explore necessary new expressions, and provide proper preparation for meaningful participation.

In addressing these responsibilities it is important to consider (1) those rituals which help us to sustain and transmit our understandings and ways, and (2) those rituals which make meaningful the crises or transitions in our lives. The first I call *rites of community.* In the Christian faith community such rituals are best exemplified by the Sunday liturgy when the community gathers to celebrate its faith. There is no more important community gathering than the Sunday liturgy which telescopes the understandings of life and the preferred ways of life of those who celebrate together. To cease worshiping is to lose faith. To transmit faith to the next generation is to include them as participants in all the community's rituals.

Characteristically, the Christian faith community has ordered its Sunday liturgy in particular ways—ways which attempt to express in structure and content the Christian faith and life. This structure has assumed many forms, each related in significant ways to history and culture, but one common expression has taken the shape of a dream which begins when the people of God gather in the name of the Lord to hear his word as contained in the Scriptures and to have that word brought into the present through preaching. The community responds to the hearing of God's word by reaffirming its historic faith. "We believe," they say, and thereby summarize the Christian faith story and establish their identity. Having its faith, the community turns naturally to a concern for God's world, expressing it in prayers of confession. These prayers are followed by prayers of confession. Week after week the community hears God's word, affirms its faith, and prays for the world, but much of life remains unchanged. The faithful need to confess their sins of omission and commission and hear God's word of acceptance. Only then can they boldly strive once again to make a proper offering, a personal and corporate commitment to live in the world as those who have received the grace of God and who intend to take up their crosses and follow after Christ. Following the offering, as disciples of Jesus Christ, they bond themselves together in community by sharing with each other the kiss of peace and celebrating the victory party of the people of God. In the joyful sharing of this thanksgiving feast with Christ they gather the strength and courage to go forth into the world as his disciples, and to that end they are commissioned and blessed.

While numerous other liturgies are possible, it is important to remember that our understandings of the Christian faith are always revealed in our rituals. It is, therefore, essential that a faith community continuously judge its ritual life by the Gospel. A corresponding search for understanding and the evaluation and reordering of ritual life are also important aspects of Christian education. Another is to prepare persons to meaningfully participate in the community's rituals.

Consider the possible significance of using the hour before the

Sunday liturgy as an opportunity for education. What if a congregation, all ages together, gathered before the morning liturgy? At this time they could welcome new persons, share fellowship together, learn about and minister to each other's needs—all of which are ways of enhancing community life. Second, the people could prepare for the morning ritual by learning hymns, responses, and other aspects of the liturgy, thereby making participation meaningful. Third, the liturgy could be enhanced if the lectionary (lessons from the Scriptures to be read and preached) was used to provide content for a series of diverse intergenerational educational experiences and discussions among all the worshipers—children, youth, and adults. By uniting learning and liturgy, Christian education could be enhanced; more important, our faith could be transmitted to our children.

The second type of ceremony, which aids us in making the transitions or changes in our lives meaningful, I call *life crisis rites.* These community rituals help us to understand and affirm the most significant moments in our lives. In terms of faith, our major life crisis rites are related to the pilgrimage of faith and its significant turning points: baptism, first communion, confirmation, ordination, and last rites. Other crisis rites—marriage, divorce, coming of age, going away to school, a new home, a move, a new job, a serious illness, retirement—can also speak to changes in our human condition in the light of Christian faith.

To understand life crisis rites properly it is helpful to realize that they each have three related phases: (1) a separation phase marked by a ceremonial withdrawal of persons from their previous status, role, or state in the community; (2) a transition phase which prepares persons through ceremonial events, training, and often ordeals for their new status, role, or state in the community; and (3) a reentry phase which, by a ceremony, establishes persons in their new status, role, or state, and reincorporates them in the community. Considering these stages in life crisis rites, it should be obvious that education can play a role, and indeed has a particularly important role to play, during the second or transition phase.

Further, education in a faith community has a special responsibility for preparing persons to participate in its life crisis liturgies. New forms of prebaptismal education are needed, as well as preparation and follow-up education for first communion and confirmation. Both the proper age or stage in life for participation (Is confirmation best celebrated with children, youth, or adults?) and the sequence or relationship between them (Should baptism, first communion, confirmation be spread out over time or united together? And in what order?) need to be understood as theological, liturgical, *and* educational issues.

My personal preference is: baptism for children at birth; first communion around first or second grade, a new "covenanting" ritual in early adolescence (to be described in chapter four); confirmation in late adolescence; ordination into Christian vocations (for all) in mid-adulthood (again see chapter four); and last rites at death. In any case, Christian education should be related to preparation for those rituals. For example, consider prebaptismal education. As soon as a couple are aware that they are to be parents (by birth or adoption) they might come before the congregation to announce that fact, be blessed, receive the prayers and support of the congregation and, most important, have godparents called forth from the congregation to help them prepare for the presence of their child. For the next several months the parents, godparents, relatives living nearby, and other children in the family might gather for a weekly supper, liturgy, and educational program to prepare spiritually for their new responsibilities and to explore how best to nurture their children in Christian faith. If the expected child should die before birth, a supportive community would exist; and if the child is born, the parents would be prepared for their child's baptism and have a supportive community to aid them in fulfilling their baptismal vows. Family life education in intergenerational groupings could then provide helpful education after baptism.

A great deal more can and ought to be said about liturgy and education, but for now let me simply express once again my contention that the liturgical and ritual aspects of life in the church need to become a major dimension of Christian education. Ritual must always be at the heart of Christian education, for in the community's liturgy, story and action merge; in worship we remember and we act in symbolic ways which bring our sacred tradition and our lives together, providing us with both meaning and motivation for daily existence. That is why, if our children are to have faith, they must worship with us.

EXPERIENCE

It is difficult to overestimate the importance of experience in the shaping of our lives. I became conscious of this fact a number of years ago when I was the member of a commission for the White House Conference on Children. The government had gathered together the most diverse group of persons with whom I had ever worked, a caricature of every type of person you can imagine: such as the young black radical from the northeast, the elderly white conservative housewife from the midwest, the middle-aged corporation executive from the south. On the first day we met, there was so much hatred and confusion I thought we would never be able to write a report, but for a year we traveled across the country and shared experiences. We witnessed American Indian children having their mouths washed out with soap for speaking their native tongue, and other atrocities and injustices. I was then asked to write a first draft of our report and was given the instructions to write something that would be approved by everyone. I was told we could not tolerate a minority report, so I struggled with that problem and all the conservative and radical persons who were to sign it. The result was a report filled with qualifying statements and hedges, and when it was read at our final meeting, the elderly white conservative housewife stood up, red faced, and exclaimed in words she surely had never uttered before, "This report isn't *radical* enough." Others agreed. It was rewritten and, like most government reports, was considered extremist and irrelevant. What had happened? We were different people; our experiences had changed us!

Similarly, the experiences we have in a community of faith are important for answering the question: Will our children have faith? We need to bring our experiences and offer them to others in our church under the judgment and inspiration of the Gospel. To engage in such reforming activity is to engage in Christian education. This conviction goes back to my first experiences in a faith community with a youth group I directed many years ago. Those were the days of large youth groups and some 298 young people were gathered in a large fellowship hall, while in the kitchen two boys were making popcorn. I began to hear shouting. "You are *not* going to put salt in the popcorn!" "I am *so* going to put salt in the popcorn!" Their voices got louder and then a body came through a wooden door. He had put salt in the popcorn! In the midst of the confusion the two boys disappeared and I was left with 298 youths wanting to know what we were going to do about them. At the time I didn't know what to do, so I said, "Let's sit down and talk about it." It was finally decided that the group would pay for the door, and the two boys would be invited back next week—to make popcorn in *two* bowls. A few days later I was in a discussion with Paul Tillich, and he said that the heart of the Gospel was being "accepted though unacceptable." That was a significant moment in my life because experience and the words of the Gospel were united.

Another transforming experience is also very clear in my memory. A few details have been changed to protect those involved. It occurred a short time ago as I was leading a youth-adult retreat.

Four hundred of us, two hundred young people and two hundred adults, had gathered to explore our faith. By evening of the first day it was discovered that over $200 was missing from people's wallets. The boys and girls were separated; hostility and anger filled the air; there were accusations and despair. After two hours I called the group together and did the only thing I knew to do; I read the incident in the temple from the Gospel According to St. John. It is the story of a woman detected in adultery (John 7:53-58). The religious leaders wanted Jesus to condemn her, but he only said, "Let the one who is faultless throw the first stone." When no one did, he said to the woman: "Has no one condemned you?" "No one, sir," she said. Jesus replied, "No more do I. You may go. Do not sin again."

After that, I prayed for God's grace among us. At the end of the prayer, the young man who had stolen the money came forward to make his confession and return the money. They were going to send him home when someone cried, "Do you want to stay?" "Yes," he mumbled. "Stay! Stay!" everyone cried. "Let us sing 'Amazing Grace'," I exclaimed, and we did. With tears running down their faces, one person after another came forward to embrace the boy.

We sometimes get so concerned about telling people things that we forget the tremendous significance of experience. I can recall another gathering at the home of the theologian Paul Tillich during my years at divinity school. We were sharing the struggles of our souls, our doubts and despair, and I suppose we expected the great theologian to say something. Instead he went to his record player and turned on the "Credo" from Bach's "B Minor Mass." The response Tillich made to our struggles with faith was to offer us the experience of listening to the historic community of faith affirm its faith in song.

Persons learn first inactively through their experience, then by imaging (stories), and last of all through the use of signs (conceptual language). For faith, it is therefore especially important to acknowledge that the most significant and fundamental form of learning is experience. Later a person may "image" that experience, and even later conceptualize it. But we begin by experiencing life in a community which seeks the good of others, then we learn the story of the Good Samaritan, and finally through reflection on our experience ("doing theology") we symbolically conceptualize the community of God in terms of love, justice, and charity. Each of these steps in learning occurs in order, and each is essential to the following step. But at the beginning is experience. A community of faith needs to be concerned about the character and nature of the experiences persons share in community. Using the community of faith as the context for Christian education encourages us to evaluate our actions and interactions in the light of the Gospel, even as we strive together to frame the sort of community life that witnesses to the action of God in our lives. We must always remember: If our children are to have Christian faith, the life they experience in the church must be a distinctive expression of the church faith story.

ACTION

Remember that it was the life of Christians in the world that converted persons to Christian faith. Too often we forget that our individual and corporate actions in society are the true test of our faith. Just as we are more apt to *act* our way into new ways of thinking than *think* our way into new ways of acting, we are more apt to learn the implications of faith through the ways we are encouraged and stimulated to act in the world than through our study of Christian ethics. Our vocation as Christians is in the world, and as children of God we are called to join God in his liberating historic actions. God is at work in the world on behalf of peace, justice, and love. To know God is to join in his history-making, and thus we need both to explore the nature and character of our individual and corporate actions in the world as aspects of our faith community's life and to make these actions a significant part of our educational ministry.

When we act under the judgment and inspiration of the Gospel to the end that God's community comes and God's will is done, we become a community of Christian faith. If our children are to have faith, our educational ministry must prepare us and stimulate us to engage in Christian actions.

As a Christian faith community we engage in personal, inter-personal, and social actions. For example, most people agree that if there are people in the community who are poor, in need of food, shelter, or care, we as Christians should respond. Indeed, through the years, personal service to those in need has exemplified the church's concern for others. Sometimes, of course, our giving of Thanksgiving baskets and Christmas presents has been patronizing and self-aggrandizing, but they were meant as acts of mercy and are to be affirmed as acts of Christian love. Nevertheless, to depend on personal actions is inadequate because of the staggering numbers in need. Interpersonal forms of action which we support, but which are conducted by professionals, are also necessary. A good example is found in our national welfare system and food stamp program. Since these methods have been often inadequate or oppressive, the church needs to take the lead in seeing that such attempts to meet need within our present economic system are developed, supported, and reformed to truly benefit the needy.

Ultimately, however, even such interpersonal actions are inad-equate to achieve economic justice and meet the needs of the poor. Social action is also, therefore, incumbent upon the church and this includes engaging in political activity to reform our economic system until justice and equity are achieved. For example, the church might take a stand on behalf of democratic socialism, and support the establishment of a guaranteed minimum income for all people and a maximum income above which no one has a right to acquire money or property. While such specific social actions may not be easily agreed upon (there is no specifically Christian economic system), I contend that the church, if it is to be a community of faith, is called by the radical nature of the Gospel to consider just such radical social actions and continuously struggle against all evil.

The church is called by God, not to be a community of cultural continuity in support of the status quo but a countercultural community of social change. Only if we come to understand our life as a faith community in terms of our actions in the world; only if we evaluate the nature and character of our personal, interpersonal, and social actions; only if we motivate and enable the church to be a community of cultural change acting on behalf of the Gospel; only then will we be a faith community worthy of Christ's name.

It may be exceedingly difficult to get a local church or denomination to agree on a plan for action, but I believe that it is essential for the church to act politically. The doctrine of the separation of church and state was created to free the church from control by the state and to secure the right of the church to judge and influence the state. To deny or ignore these rights and responsibilities is to misunderstand and be unfaithful to the church's mission. No one ever said that this would be easy, but a proper and adequate educational ministry should equip, motivate, and aid the church in fulfilling its corporate mission in the world.

However, one warning! Too often the church, acting on its emotions and sense of good will, has been mindless; the results have been disastrous. There is no alternative for serious study and intellectual investigation. Too often religious education has neglected its responsibility to aid the community in securing the facts, investigating alternative actions and their consequences, and designing political strategies. Social action without knowledge and hard-nosed thinking is irresponsible. The church needs to train its people to *think* politically, socially, economically, theologically, and ethically.

Religious education cannot place those needs too high on its list of priorities.

Still, as it reflects on action as an aspect of its educational ministry, the church has yet another related responsibility. Each of us spends our daily life engaged in some activity; we need help in turning jobs into vocations, and our daily decisions into ethical decisions informed by Christian faith. Christian education needs to address such needs.

Finally, an important word: We face no greater evil in society than racism, to which every institution, the church included, continues to contribute. The educational ministry of the church must help us to understand how we participate in this injustice and then equip and motivate us to effect change in the institutions of which we are a part. Now as always the church is challenged to tell its story to the world by what it stands for and what it does. Our educational ministry must assist us in doing just that. Our children will have faith, only if we do.

TESTING COMMUNITY

Historically, all education has vacillated between three concerns: knowledge, persons, and society. Consider for a moment how we train leaders for the church's ministry. Divinity schools or seminaries have sometimes emphasized one or another of these three foci in their curriculum. When a concern for "knowledge" has dominated, they have focused on either a core of knowledge and/or the disciplines of biblical studies, church history, theology, and ethics. When a concern for "persons" has dominated, they have focused on the spiritual development and faith of their students. And when a concern for "society" has dominated, they have focused on the vocation of ministry and such specific skills as preaching, counseling, or administration (rarely education).

While most seminaries include all three foci in their curriculum rhetoric, one or another has usually assumed greater worth. For example, while a core of knowledge once dominated our seminary curricula, the trend now is moving to skills for ministry. A similar analysis can be made of education in the church. However, it is most important to affirm that all three are equally essential for Christian education. We cannot afford to let one or another dominate or be ignored. Our rituals, our experiences in the church, and our individual and corporate actions in the world need to be judged and inspired by (1) how well they are informed by and express our Christian tradition, (2) how well they enhance and sustain our spiritual lives, and (3) how well they equip and motivate us for action in the world. If our children are to have faith, Christian education must be whole. That means making sure that a Christian understanding of the tradition, persons, and society influences and is expressed in the community's rituals, experiences, and actions in the world.

THE TRADITION

A community of faith is essentially a community interacting with a living tradition. The tradition we bear as a faith community is essentially and primarily a story of God's mighty deeds and actions in history. The Christian story is a story about vision. In the beginning God has a vision of a world at one with itself, a world of peace, justice, freedom, equity, whole community, and the well-being of all. It is the world God intends.

God creates persons in his image, historic actors who he intends will live in and for his vision. But God also grants persons the freedom to say yes or no to his vision. And so the plot thickens. We humans are more interested in our visions than God's vision. We create systems ("principalities and powers") which benefit some of us but not all of us. As a result of our own selfish actions we become isolated from nature, ourselves, each other, and God.

But God persists in seeking after us. God calls a community into being to witness to his vision. And he takes the side of those who are either kept outside or oppressed by the systems we humans create. God, biased toward the hurt and the have-nots, acts on their behalf that his vision might be realized. God liberated the slaves in Egypt, patiently pulled them toward his vision, and established a covenant with them to live as his visionary community. Still, it doesn't work, for as soon as we humans begin to receive the blessings of God's vision we act to keep those blessings for ourselves alone. God continues to raise up prophets to remind us of his intentions for his world, and a faithful remnant keeps the story of God's vision alive.

Nevertheless, it is as if we are in bondage to the social forces, to the political, economic, and social systems we have built. Over and over again some individuals catch a glimpse of God's vision and commit their lives to its realization; yet that vision still remains a lost dream. So God makes a decision and God acts again, enters our human condition, becomes incarnate in Jesus of Nazareth— the storyteller, doer of deeds, healer of hurts, advocate of the outsider, liberator of the oppressed. Through Jesus the good news is announced: God's community has come. In the absurdity and foolishness of the cross, God acts to liberate us from bondage to the principalities and powers. Nothing—no social, political, or economic power—can hold us any longer. So, on Easter morning the disciples behold the dawn of God's coming community. Love using power has overcome oppression.

Yet the dawn of hope is not yet the high noon of God's community come on earth. Darkness still covers much of the land, people are still oppressed, wars continue, poverty and hunger prevail, injustice is perpetuated, and the mass of humanity is still marginal to God's promise. Many of us who claim the name Christian

continue to frustrate God's vision and live as if we do not understand the implications of the Gospel. We bless our individualism
and competition, we say this is the best of all possible worlds, we
justify our way of life.

God calls prophets forth to remind us of his vision and the radical demands it places on our lives. The Gospel itself judges and
inspires us. Here and there some live according to God's will and
for God's coming community. Each week the community of faith
gathers to celebrate its hope, to point to the signs of God's coming
community, to announce that we are liberated from the principalities and powers, and to stimulate us to act with God for his vision.

The church is the bearer of that story. And when that story
becomes our story we will know what the name Christian means.
Education is concerned that the story be known and owned; it is
concerned that this story be understood and applied. We had better
agree on the story, for it needs to be expressed in our individual
and corporate lives. It is a story that needs to be told and made
incarnate in the life of a faith community. But that presents us with
a difficulty, for we have all too often been willing to turn the story
into dogmas and doctrines that lack charisma and power. Worse
than that, we have continued either to tell only preferred parts of
the story or to misinterpret the story when it doesn't benefit us,
turning the Gospel into an opiate of personal piety and ignoring its
call to social liberation.

We too easily forget that the message of the prophet Isaiah is
delivered to a community, a people, and not an individual or one
particular group. We ignore the fact that his message is a message
to a people who have been in bondage and oppression, waiting for a
redemptive act of God. To the have-nots, the oppressed, repressed,
depressed, and suppressed people of the world, God speaks in the
prophet Isaiah a word of comfort (Isaiah 40). In our sin we misunderstand that message and do not hear its word of judgment on
the rest of us. Of course, it is a message of judgment tempered by

mercy, but mercy which requires repentance and a changed life. God is putting things right in his world, bringing to fruition his visionary community, and we are called to join God in his revolutionary historic social activity. That is the story we have to tell; that is the story that needs to judge and inspire every aspect of our life. How we interpret and apply that story is also important. It would be well for us to realize that the Bible is "poetry plus" and not "science minus." For too long we have permitted and encouraged only one limited means or interpretation.

Two and a half centuries ago there was a struggle within the faculty at St. Thomas School in Leipzig between the cantor of the school, J. S. Bach, and the new rector, J. A. Ernesti, a pioneer in the literary historical criticism of the Bible. Bach believed that the Scriptures could best be understood and interpreted through the use of music and worship, while Ernesti believed that reason dictated a more scholarly approach to biblical interpretation. Today we desperately need to remind ourselves that *both* the artistic and the rationalistic perspectives have value, and that a return to congregational singing of the St. Matthew Passion is as important for understanding and interpreting the story of our faith as the critical literary-historical study of its message. In any case the tradition must judge, inform, and inspire every aspect of our lives, and Christian education must see that we come to know, understand, interpret, live, and act that tradition if our children are to have faith.

PERSONS

There are days when it appears as if some professional educators believe that human beings are only minds. Mirroring the current emphasis in psychology and pedagogy, Christian educators have tended to emphasize cognition and thinking. We have, it seems, turned faith into a way of knowing and nothing else. Of course knowing is important and thinking is important; in light of the anti-intellectualism that has infected so much of church life, that cannot be overemphasized. Nevertheless, thinking is not sufficient in and of itself. I would like to defend the point that we are essentially agents, historic actors whose lives are best understood as a gestalt of thinking, feeling, and willing. We are created to act in the world as spiritual beings and that is why we are called to live lives of prayer—the spiritual life—through continual adoration, confession, petition, intercession, and thanksgiving.

Adoration, as I understand it, is focusing our lives upon God. It is the life of the dreamer and visionary that makes it possible to view every aspect of life as a miracle. *Confession* is the continual self-examination of our personal and social lives in the presence of God; it is living under the judgment of God's will. *Petition and intercession* are bringing our desires for self and others in line with God's desires or attuning our hearts and minds and wills to that of God. *Thanksgiving* is our active daily expression of gratitude to God for his continuing action in history, a celebrative awareness of God's actions in our midst.

We are told by Jesus to pray without ceasing, but surely that does not mean to live on our knees uttering words to God. Rather, prayer is living consciously in the presence of a God who acts in history through persons and communities to establish his community of love, power, and justice. Prayer involves living with a conscious awareness of God's presence, of uniting our wills with God's in common reflective action. Prayer is a radical ethical activity, a passionate action that results from both intuitive and intellectual activity.

Two modes of consciousness are possible for human beings. One is intellectual and focused on the universal and the abstract, and is characterized by verbal, linear, conceptual, and analytical activities. The other is intuitional and focuses on the syncretic and the experiential, and is characterized by nonverbal, creative, nonlinear, relational activities. The development and integration of both modes of consciousness is essential to the spiritual life.

Numerous examples of the spiritual life in the Bible support such understanding. Operating from that perspective, the prophets (understanding history as the place of God's creativity) used their intuitive powers to hear the voice of God, and their intellects to reflect on God's word so they might act with God in history.

Moses' intuitive experience with the burning bush led him to reflect on his life and bring to his people a vision and message of liberation. The intuitive awareness of Christ's presence in the breaking of the bread at Emmaus led the disciples to lives of radical apostleship. None of these experiences or their resulting acts were purely rational or intuitional. Each represents a worldly intuitive experience which, through the use of the intellect, led to new sorts of moral behavior.

To understand persons as thinking, feeling, and willing historical actors is to support the growth and development of a person's intellectual and intuitive skills as well as his or her historical awareness. Christian education requires that we help persons regain their God-given ability to wonder and create; to dream and fantasize, imagine and envision; to sing, paint, dance, and act. It requires a recovery of our natural ability for ecstasy; our appreciation of the new, the marvelous, the mysterious; and a sensual and kinesthetic awareness. It requires a recovery of our God-given talent to express ourselves emotionally and nonverbally.

Concern for the religious affections must once again become a central concern of church education, and participation in the arts must become an essential focus of our educational ministries. We need also to focus on the development of historical awareness, and that will not be easy. We live in a historical time because we have been taught our history as a meaningless collection of dates, names, and places. Few of us are conscious of a meaningful past, and most of us consider the past we do recall as irrelevant to the present. As a result we are trapped in the present. Storytelling needs to become a natural and central part of church life, and we must learn to tell God's story as *our* story. No longer can we explain how some Israelites were once in bondage in Egypt and how God saved them. (Who cares?) Instead we need to explain how *we* were once oppressed in Egypt and how God liberated *us*. We must again become a history-bearing community of faith and a storytelling people who seek to communicate God's story as our story. We need to remember that as persons we are actors in history; indeed faith is action and our faith is best revealed in our actions. If our children are to have faith, every aspect of church life must be inspired, judged, and informed by how well it nurtures our spiritual lives as thinking, feeling, willing people of God who act individually and corporately in the world to reveal the Gospel.

SOCIETY

Church education has most often vacillated between a concern for persons and a concern for tradition. We typically forget that we are corporate selves called to live in but not of the world. The community of faith has a vocation as a countercultural community and not as a mirror of the society, for it is called to give witness through word and deed to an alternative to life as it is.

In order for us to take our vocation in the world seriously, we need visions, hope, and power. And we need to ask to what extent our rituals, our experiences in the community of faith, and our action in the world express God's vision for humanity. Our society, the church included, is largely without visions, which means without clear and adequate goals. And thus the question—Will our children have faith?—is especially pertinent. Without visions the people perish, but God has given us a vision expressed by the Hebrew word *Shalom* and in the metaphor of the kingdom—or better, the community—of God: It is life in the world characterized by well-being, peace, liberation, justice, and whole community. The people of God are called to live for this vision and the church's educational ministry is given the responsibility of transmitting and sustaining that vision and enhancing its understanding.

Of course it is not enough to have visions; we need to have hope of their realization. Christian hope boldly and confidently affirms that, despite all evidence to the contrary, God's community has come, is coming, and will come in all its glory. To live and die for that vision makes sense and is worth any price. To live in the hope of the Gospel is to search for where God is acting in the world and join God in his activity. Hope founded in Christ has no alternative but to engage in social action that challenges the evils of society and creates more human alternatives. Of course only God will establish God's community in God's good time, but we are called to act faithfully, to struggle against all evil, and to live in hope. That may mean moving from one human reform to another, always judging the inadequacies of our last reform and striving for a better alternative. Christian education needs to help us live in and for that hope which inspires the continual struggle for justice and equity no matter what the odds or disappointments.

In addition to visions and hope we also need power—the wisdom, skills, know-how, and motivation—to act politically, socially, and economically in the world. Christian education needs to have as a primary responsibility the equipment and motivation of the people of God for corporate action in the world. We must never forget that our Christian vocation is in the world and that Christian educators must be engaged in helping us acquire the skills necessary to be responsible political and social agents. No aspects of our educational ministry have been more neglected. One of the greatest challenges facing Christian education is in enabling the church to be a witnessing community of faith. Only if we see that task as equally as important as our concern for the tradition and the spiritual lives of persons will our educational ministry fulfill its vocation and our children have faith.

CONCLUSION

Using the radical nature and character of a faith community as the context or place for Christian education means using every aspect of our church's life for education—our rituals and preparation for participation, the experiences we have and provide within the community of faith, and the individual and corporate actions we inspire and equip persons to engage in. It means examining and judging our total life as a community of faith to see how well we live and transmit our Christian story or tradition, how well we minister to the total needs of whole persons in community, and how well we prepare and motivate individuals and communities to act on behalf of God's coming community in the world. This means understanding religious education in terms of a continuing struggle to reform the church.

If we make our life in a community of faith the context of Christian education, it will mean living each day under the judgment and inspiration of the Gospel to the end that God's community comes and God's will is done. The willingness to affirm and accept this understanding is the challenge of Christian education today; it is also the basis for an answer to the question: Will our children have faith?

UPDATE

I am a bit clearer now on the necessary context in which Christian nurture can take place, namely, a community of faith with these particular characteristics:

1. A community of faith has a common story, and its life is shaped by that story. Stories form community, and it is the biblical story that must shape the church's life by becoming its story.

2. A community of faith has a common authority. It agrees on its author, its source for discerning the will of God. Unless there is an agreed-upon authority and a common knowledge of how that authority operates in aiding us to discern and make decisions, there is nothing to hold us together when we differ, nor is there a means for reconciling differences and reaching a new consensus.

3. A community of faith has common rituals around which it celebrates and orders its life. As repetitive symbolic actions (word-and-deed acts) that express its sacred story, rituals *In Search of Community* 75 provide the primary influence in shaping faith, character, and consciousness. They also make possible harmonious communal life and help people to make meaningful transitions in their lives.

4. A community of faith has a common life that is more like a familial community than an institution. That is, it focuses its concerns on every aspect of human life and not solely on religious matters; it continuously engages the whole personality of people, and not just some aspect of it, for a period of time; it is bound together by a covenant that calls us to do whatever love demands to keep us united, rather than by a contract in which the terms are "If you do A, I will do

B"; it orders its life by custom (habits of the heart) rather than
by laws and rules; and the worth of its members is in their
being and not in their contributions or participation. When
conflicts erupt, a community of faith views these differences
as a healthy and normal part of its life and allows for honest
dialogue as part of the conflict-resolution process, which
takes both the issue and the relationships seriously.

5. A community of faith lives for an end beyond itself and
   its own survival. This implies that intimacy cannot be its
   goal, for if it is, it will exclude people who are different.
   Instead a community of faith will be able to bind together
   very different kinds of people because of a commitment to a
   common end and not simply because they like one another.

6. A community of faith values diversity. This implies that the
   community welcomes into its midst persons of different ages,
   cultures, social class, and racial and ethnic backgrounds.
   Such a community sees the positive value of differences and
   encourages their expressions in daily life.

The Trinity provides us with a model of Christian community, the
mystery that three divine persons can be in a perfect communion of
love. It is a model of church not as a political or social ideal or the
sort of community that will attract Baby Boomers or Generation X
but is a model of the church that is theological at its core. The concept of the Trinity offers us an image of communal life constituted
in a people with a united mind, heart, and will, bound together in
perfect love, yet remaining differentiated persons. It is a community in which people find themselves in what others receive from
them. This trinitarian relationship is not autonomous, for none of
the three persons claims any rights from the other. It is a theono-
mous relationship in which the three are lovers who, while forever
free actors, are never free from each other. Their life together is for
privilege and responsibility, not for advantage or rights.

I am surer than ever of the primary role of ritual in Christian formation. In 1925, Willard Sperry, the dean of the Harvard Divinity School and campus minister for Harvard University, wrote *Reality in Worship* (New York: Macmillan Co., p. 159ff). In a chapter entitled "The Occasion and Intention of Public Worship," he suggested that the church shares with many other institutions common tasks that are religious in nature and that many of these activities are better done by institutions other than the church; for example, the administration of hospitals and schools. However, he contended, the one unique contribution of the church is its cultic life. While the work of the church is real and intelligible through the life and actions of its members, whenever and wherever people meet together avowedly to address themselves to the act of liturgy, there the church is clearly defined. Liturgy is the original and distinctive task, the primary responsibility of the church. Everything else may be conceded, compromised, shared, and even relinquished. However, so long as the church invites people to worship God and provides a credible vehicle for liturgy, it need not question its place, mission, and influence in the world. If it loses faith in liturgy, is thoughtless in the ordering of liturgy, or is careless in the conduct of liturgy, it need not look elsewhere to find vitality: it is dead at its heart.

Within secular culture there are numerous rites that are intended to shape the community's worldview and value system. They, too, are repetitive, symbolic actions expressive of the community's ways. The dominant secular rites are spectator sports intended to support individualism (baseball is popular, and in such team-oriented sports we give a most valuable player award), aggression (the most popular sports are the most violent), competition (ties are considered unsatisfactory; someone needs to win and cooperation is understood as being only in terms of one's own team in order to beat another team) and nationalism (singing the national anthem before each game). Advertising is a form of cultural rite that supports an economic system based on self-interest and consumption. These rites and others constantly attempt to enculturate us to particular ways that explain why, when persons entered the catechumenate in the early church to be formed as Christians, they were no longer permitted to attend public spectator sports. If we are to be formed as Christians, we must take our Christian rites seriously. This means making participation in the church's liturgies the heart of formation.

Liturgy, a people's social behavior, has two dimensions in cultic life (ritual worship) and daily life. In theory they are directly related to each other. Nevertheless, sometimes there is a split between worship and our lives. Therefore, whenever the church believes that it is not being as faithful as it ought to be, it engages in a reform of its worship. While the reasons for the split between worship and our daily lives are numerous, let me mention five:

1. People come to church to escape life's problems rather than to be engaged and transformed to face them creatively.

2. The rituals of society are taken more seriously than those of the church, and we are more influenced by them.

3. Our rituals are either too unrelated to our culture or too much in harmony with it.

4. Our ritual life is too intellectual. We have forgotten that good ritual is concerned with the intuitive way of thinking and being and is best composed in the arts, drama, music, body movement, poetry, and the visual arts.

5. We have ignored the "hidden curriculum" of our rituals (what we really communicate in spite of our intentions) and so we engage in symbolic acts that are contrary to our moral intentions. For example, we kneel at the end of the liturgy after we have been sent forth to love and serve.

And last, writing today, I would now put more emphasis on the spiritual life and the importance of the arts and of beauty understood as a revelation of the presence (priestly) or absence (prophetic) of truth and goodness.

The spiritual life is ordinary everyday life, lived in an ever-deepening and loving relationship with God and thereby lived in an ever-deepening and loving relationship with self (the self in the image and likeness of God), all other people, and creation itself—the moral life. The spiritual life comes first. The test of its faithfulness is the moral life. We cannot have a healthy relationship with God and have an unhealthy relationship with self, neighbors, or nature. However, if we are to have a healthy relationship with self, neighbors, or nature, we will need to first nurture the spiritual life. The most important means for doing so is to enhance and enliven the intuitive way of thinking and knowing through participation in the arts—music, visual arts, drama, dance, and so on. This spiritual life needs to become the heart of our efforts to make Christians. We humans have only one end for our lives—to grow into a loving relationship with God; all else is to be means to that end.

CHAPTER FOUR

Life Together

The central question is: How can the community educate for true and living faith and not merely for conformity to the accepted norms of belief and conduct within the nurturing fellowship?
Philip H. Phenix

In response to the question asked by this book, it is easier to name the context for Christian education than it is to name the means. Instruction—teaching and learning—is not sufficient. But what are the alternatives? In *Generation to Generation* I introduced the concept "intentional socialization." I still believe it is a helpful concept, but as a result of theological reflections I have become increasingly wary of its use. Intentional socialization implies that someone does something to someone else. While the concept wisely broadens the context of Christian education to include every aspect of life in the church and makes us more mindful of our "hidden curriculum," it still gives the impression that we can and ought to be concerned about determining the life and faith of another. That, I want to question!

Perhaps it would be better to begin with the question: What does it mean to be Christian together? Such a question turns our attention from behavioral objectives for others to the character and quality of life lived together in a community of faith. Christian faith implies the need to focus on the mutuality of our engagements with each other, thereby eliminating all categories such as teacher and student, adult (the one who knows) and child (the one who needs to know), socializer and socializee. For these reasons, I have chosen the word "enculturation" to characterize educational method in a faith community.

While much socialization literature has a tendency to emphasize how the environment, experiences, and actions of others influence us, enculturation emphasizes the process of interaction between and among persons of all ages. It focuses on the interactive experiences and environments within which persons act to acquire, sustain, change, and transmit their understandings and ways. In enculturation one person is not understood as the actor and another the acted upon, but rather both act, both initiate action, and both react. It is the nature, character, and quality of these interactive experiences among people of all ages within a community of faith that best describes the means of Christian education.

While most instructional literature has a tendency to emphasize imparting knowledge or skill to another person or the deliberate attempt to produce specific desired learning outcomes in another, enculturation emphasizes what one person has to bring to another and the dialogical relationship between equals.

The language of instruction does not encourage us to think in terms of interaction. Therefore, some people act as if all essential knowledge and human possibility are within us at birth. They choose to remove themselves and as many other barriers to maturation as possible in order to encourage a person's natural growth to fulfillment. Others act as if a person at birth is an empty vessel which is to be filled, and they, therefore, must assume responsibility for what that person should be and know. Of course these are exaggerations, but they do explain and describe, even if in extreme terms, the varied assumptions and behavior of some educators.

Neither view, in my opinion, is adequate from either a theological or pedagogical perspective. In one important sense, each of us has faith at birth; it is not, therefore, given to us by others. Still our faith requires that we interact with other faithing selves to actualize itself and to develop its character and content. To understand faith and its content we need to focus our attention on the experiences of interaction between and among faithing persons in a self-conscious tradition bearing community of faith. What is important is not what we strive to give to another, but what we share and the various ways we strive to be Christian together within a community of faith.

In the 50s and 60s a few religious educators affirmed a similar position. They spoke of the language of relationships, dialogical education, and experiential learning. They spoke of life together in community. But the schooling-instructional paradigm prevented their position from receiving a fair hearing.

Of course, the idea was not new to them. Much earlier, John Dewey had defended a developmental-interactional view of education which stressed the importance of experiences that foster interaction between persons and their environment. Indeed, anthropologists interested in learning have always spoken of interactions between persons and their communities. And even the teachers of the early Sunday school movement shared similar convictions.

In 1905 John Vincent, the great Methodist leader of the Sunday school movement, then in his later years, gave an address at the Eleventh International Sunday School Convention in Toronto, Canada. It was entitled "A Forward Look for the Sunday School," and he began with an important observation, namely, that it is possible to make too much of method, of recent educational theory, of curricula, teaching, and intellectual training. He explained that the Sunday school, in its desire to gratify modern education, was in danger of making a blunder and of sacrificing good things that are old. Then Vincent made a prediction: In the future the Sunday school will be less like a school and more like a home. Its program will focus on conversation and the interaction of people rather than the academic study of the Bible or theology. The Sunday school will be a place where friends deeply concerned about Christian faith will gather to share life together.

In 1816 J. A. James wrote *The Sunday School Teacher's Guide.* He opened with the conviction that teaching religion is something more than giving instruction. He further explained that the accumulation of biblical facts and figures and the memorization of passages of Scripture are an insignificant part of religious education, and that teaching is not to be an end in itself but a means to an end. James went on to describe the Sunday schools he knew best, first telling of children, youth, and adults preparing for and celebrating special occasions, such as Christmas, Easter, Thanksgiving, Missionary Day, and Decision Day. In a chapter entitled "We Learn By Doing," he described life in the Sunday school and included plays and musicals, games, hikes and hunts, parties and picnics, social service projects and community activities in which children, youth, parents, and grandparents participated together. The function of the Sunday school, with its variety of programs, was to give persons an opportunity to share life with other faithful selves, to experience the faith in community, to learn the Christian story and to engage in Christian actions. The key to these Sunday schools was not curriculum, teaching, learning strategies, or organization; it was people in community.

Benjamin Jacob, the Baptist layman who helped to transform the Sunday school into a worldwide movement, spoke of teaching as leading others by example on the road to spiritual maturity.

Children, he pointed out, may or may not study their Bibles as diligently as desired, but they will study the lives of the adults they meet in the church. And so teachers must be models of what they desire others to become; they are to be spirited mentors and not instructors.

In 1887 John Vincent wrote *The Modern Sunday School,* in which he described the Sunday school as a modern title for an ancient and apostolic service of the church. It is, he explained, a school first and foremost for disciples and it is a place where persons share their faith with each other. Vincent presented a variety of roles a teacher might play: he can entertain his pupils and keep them happy; he can work at winning their admiration; he can make them into good scholars who know the Bible and the church's doctrines. Vincent accepted none of these. Instead, he listed the spiritual qualities needed by teachers so that they may share their faith and thus aid in the spiritual growth and development of those they meet. A number of years later Senabaugh contended in *The Small Church School* that not just anyone can teach, for religion is caught more than taught and we cannot teach what we do not know and believe. Religion, he said, is an experience, and we cannot communicate anything that we have not verified. The teacher may teach about Christianity, but if he is to communicate Christ he must live in fellowship with him.

The old Sunday school appears to have cared most about creating an environment where people could be Christian together and where persons could experience Christian faith and see it witnessed to in the lives of significant people. The old Sunday school seemed to be aware of the importance of the affections, of storytelling, of experience, of community sharing, and of role models. While many of these concerns remain in the rhetoric of the modern church school movement, we seem to have created an institution more concerned with teaching strategies, instructional gimmicks, and curricular resources than with spiritual mentors; more concerned with age-graded classes for cognitive growth than with communities concerned with the affections; more concerned with the goals of knowing about the Bible, theology, and church history than with communities sharing, experiencing, and acting together in faith.

Verbal language, both spoken and written, has dominated Christian education for too long. Perhaps as far as Christian faith is concerned, we have attached too literal an interpretation to the primacy of the word. By sanctifying the oral and verbal traditions, we have lost something of the richness of the early church where the great truths of the community were enshrined in shared experience.

At the turn of the century, W. G. E. Cunnyngham wrote *Sunday School.* His main point was this: If one does not believe a person, one will not believe what that person says. Children, he continued, are close observers of character. They deal with the concrete and not the abstract; with them, actions speak louder than words.

The challenge facing the church is in the bland, unconverted, ignorant lives of its members. Until adults in the church are knowledgeable in their faith, have experienced the transforming power of the Gospel, live radical lives characteristic of the disciples of Jesus Christ, no new curriculum, no new insights on learning, no new teacher-training programs, and no new educational technology will save us.

Remember the parables of Jesus about the hidden treasure and the pearl of great price? The question we need to ask is this: Do I have in my experience anything to offer for which anyone would conceivably want to sell all they have to obtain? The quality of our faith will always reveal what we *are.* And what we *are* will in the end determine the value and effect of what we do. We must, therefore, pay attention first of all to ourselves.

The language of instruction can too easily lead us astray. It encourages us to be concerned for what we want our pupils to be or become. When we think "instruction," we focus our attention on what we want someone else to know, what we want someone else to feel, or how we want someone else to behave. We establish learning objectives for others, while parents legitimately ask us when we are going to teach their child about the Bible or what Christians believe or what is right and wrong.

But subject matter is not the issue; object matter is! As Albert Camus once said, if a thought is to change the world, it must first change the life of the person who carries it; it must become an example. The important questions are simply, but profoundly: What do I have to bring to another? What is truly mine that I have to share with others?

The most important questions a person can ask are: How can I be what I say I am? How can I live what I profess? There ought to be some identifiable difference between the person who claims the name of Christ and someone who denies him. If we truly are in Christ there should be qualities, characteristics, dispositions, and understandings discernible in our inner and outward lives. There is no shadow of doubt in the New Testament that a professed Christian should be able to be known as such. Christian faith, says St. Paul in his letter to the Galatians (5:13-26), involves a fundamental change at the core of our being, a change brought about by the nature of our relationship to Christ and by the inner presence of the Holy Spirit. Nobody can rejoice in Christ and then go and do just as he pleases. There is a life appropriate to our calling. There are fruits of the spirit that are indicators of Christian faith.

The Christian faith invites women and men to a new level of existence, and the Gospel announces that this radically different sort of life is possible. But if we who proclaim the Gospel do not live it, then what? The answer to this question explains why enculturation—the interactions in community between faithful persons—is more adequate than instruction for understanding educational method in a faith community. Namely because the process of enculturation encourages us to consider our own faith and life with others. Instruction tends to encourage us to focus on the faith and life of the other, and therefore avoids the issue of how faith is sustained and transmitted.

A current issue facing Christian ethics may provide an interesting set of insights for understanding what is at stake in the choice between instruction and enculturation. It can be stated in this way: At a time when medical knowledge enables doctors to save and sustain life as never before, the value of doing so is increasingly questioned. What should we do with hopeless cases of people not imminently dying but so ill or handicapped or distraught as to face meaningless lives that are not worth living?

There are two alternative ways of viewing this problem: One can be described as the "quality-of-life" view and the other the "equality-of-life" view. The first encourages us to base our decisions to maintain life on utilitarian grounds such as social worth, to equate human dignity with control, to believe that to be dependent is to be less than human, and to maintain that certain forms of life are not human. The second asserts that life is a basic right of all, a right not to be qualified by another's assessment of the quality of any individual's life. Life itself confers dignity; life itself has worth. The living are equal in that each has worth as a human being. Life itself has value, and intentionally destroying it is morally wrong. The position maintains that the only question to be raised is whether or not we are indeed loving God and loving our neighbor. The moral question is not whether or not the other is a person, but whether we are the kinds of persons who will care for them without doubting their worth.

My personal conviction is that the second position is Christian. And I contend that a similar issue faces us when we decide on a method for Christian education. Under the rubrics of teaching and learning, or socialization, we have tended to emphasize our responsibility for deciding what another should know, be, and do. We want to know how we can make others into Christians, how we can put information about Christianity into their heads, how we can provide others with Christian experience, or how we can modify others' behavior until they act as we believe Christians should act.

We need a new way of thinking about educational method, a way that emphasizes what *we* know, what *we* are and what *we* do. It is a way that forces us to focus on ourselves and not on the other. We cannot, as Christians, busy ourselves with deciding on the quality of another's life. We need to affirm the equality of all lives, and when we do, we shall begin to have an alternative understanding of educational method. Christian education needs to affirm the value of each life as equal before God. Our responsibility is to make our own life consistent with our calling and to share that life with others. We need to acknowledge not only the worth of others, but our need of their life and witness for our own growth in faith.

Shared experience, storytelling, celebration, action, and reflection between and among equal "faithing" selves within a community of faith best help us understand how faith is transmitted, expanded, and sustained. And so I contend that understanding the processes of *interaction* in community between "faithing" selves— what I have called enculturation— is the best way to understand educational method in a faith community.

FAITH AND ITS EXPANSION

Faith, as I have used the word, is a verb. Faith is a way of behaving which involves knowing, being, and willing. The content of faith is best described in terms of our worldview and value system, but faith itself is something we do. Faith is an action. It results from our actions with others, it changes and expands through our actions with others, and it expresses itself daily in our actions with others.

After reflection on my own and others' faith pilgrimages, I have been able to describe four distinctive styles of faith. This conceptualization is not original, and I was first influenced to think about

a stage theory for the development of faith through the important research of my friend James Fowler. Since we began commu-
nicating, however, I have proceeded in directions for which only
I can be held responsible. Nevertheless, I do need and want to
acknowledge my early debt, and to suggest that Fowler's research
may necessitate significant changes in my own ideas.

At this point, I am prepared to suggest that faith (understood
as a way of behaving) can, if provided with the proper interactive experiences, expand through four distinctive *styles* of faith.
Each style of faith to be described is a generalization, and none are
meant to be boxes into which persons are placed; neither are they
to be used as judgments upon ourselves or others. I have named the
first style of faith, *experienced faith;* the second, *affiliative faith;*
the third, *searching faith;* and the fourth, *owned faith.* I have tried
many ways to describe the relationship between these styles of faith
and the best I've found, though still inadequate, is drawn from the
analogy of a tree.

First, a tree with one ring is as much a tree as a tree with four
rings. A tree in its first year is a complete and whole tree, and a
tree with three rings is not a better tree but only an expanded tree.
In a similar way, one style of faith is not a better or greater faith
than another. Experienced faith, the first identifiable style, is complete and whole faith. One seeks to act with other faithing selves
in community and hence to expand into new styles of faith, not so
as to possess better or greater faith, but only to fulfill one's faith
potential.

Second, a tree grows if the proper environment is provided, and
if such an environment is lacking, the tree becomes arrested in its
expansion until the proper environment exists. Each tree, however,
does its own "growing" and has its own unique characteristics.
Similarly, we expand from one style faith to another only if the
proper environment, experiences, and interactions are present; and
if they are not, then our expansion of faith is arrested. Of course

no style of faith is natural to any particular age and everyone can expand into a new style providing the proper interactions with other faithing souls are present.

Third, a tree acquires one ring at a time in a slow and gradual manner. We do not see that expansion, although we do see the results, and surely we are aware that you cannot skip rings, moving from a one-ring to a three-ring tree. The same is true of faith. We expand from one style of faith to another slowly and gradually (it cannot be rushed), adding one style at a time in an orderly process over time.

Fourth, as a tree grows, it does not eliminate rings but adds each ring to the ones before, always maintaining all the previous rings as it expands. It is the same with faith. As we expand in faith we do not leave one style of faith behind to acquire a new style but, on the contrary, each new style is added to the previous ones. We do not outgrow a style of faith and its needs but expand it by adding new elements and new needs. Indeed, if the needs of an earlier style of faith cease to be met, persons have a tendency to return to that earlier style of faith. Once, however, these needs are again satisfied persons return to their farthest expanded style of faith.

Faith is an action which includes thinking, feeling, and willing and it is transmitted, sustained, and expanded through our interactions with other faithing selves in a community of faith. To describe each style of faith is to understand the faith pilgrimage possible for us all. To those styles of faith we turn now.

EXPERIENCED FAITH

No one can determine another's faith and no one can give another faith, but we can be faithful and share our life and our faith with another. Others, regardless of age, can do the same with us, and through this sharing we each sustain, transmit, and expand our faith.

During the preschool and early childhood years, children typically act with "experienced faith." That is to say faith is first experienced enactively. To understand this style of faith we need to remember that children initiate action and respond to our actions. The child explores and tests, imagines and creates, observes and copies, experiences and reacts. Children's actions influence those with whom they interact, and the actions of others influence them. Their acts provide a mirror and a test for those with whom they interact. Not only children live by experienced faith, of course, and while this style of faith represents the earliest style, its characteristics are important and foundational to persons throughout their lives. For example, just as children need to be hugged, caressed, and stroked, so do adults. Regretfully, we seem to have forgotten that and, as a result, adolescent and adult "skin hunger" needs are met by antisocial punching and jabbing. Basic and continuing needs are denied because we have not found socially acceptable ways to affirm hugs between persons of the same and opposite sex. Similarly, throughout our lives, we need to take seriously the needs of experienced faith and, like the child, we need to act in ways that explore and test, observe and copy, imagine and create, experience and react.

Experience is foundational to faith. A person first learns Christ not as a theological affirmation but as an affective experience. For children and adults, it is not so much the words we hear spoken that matter most, but the experiences we have which are connected with those words. Language and experience are interrelated. Experiences of trust, love, and acceptance are important to Christian faith and, regardless of age, the need is always present for experiences consistent with the meanings we attribute to our words. If a person is "used" whenever the word love is spoken, the word love takes on that meaning for the person. A new definition can be learned, but the power of the word will be related to the experiences of the word. That explains why we are called to be doers of the word and not hearers only. As the apostle James writes: " 'Here is one who claims to have faith and another who points to his deeds.' To which I reply: 'Prove to me that this faith you speak of is real though not accompanied by deeds, and by my deeds I will prove to you my faith' " (2:18). We experience and express faith through our interactions with others. The meaning of our vocabulary of faith is directly related to our experience with the words spoken to express that faith.

To be concerned about others' faith is to share our faith with them in word and deed, and to permit them to share their faith with us in similar ways. We can share and respond, but the character of another person's faith cannot be determined. What we can do is provide an environment of sharing and interaction between faithing selves. The responsibility of Christian parents is to endeavor to be Christian with their children, and the responsibility of all Christians is to strive to be Christian with all others. God makes himself known through his word—his actions.

God has not waited to be discovered, but has taken the initiative and addressed his word to humankind through his deeds. In Jesus Christ, the word became flesh. God established the criteria by which we may recognize and understand the word and deed of God in many other and unexpected ways; but for Christian faith, word and deed are never separated.

Experienced faith, therefore, results from our interactions with other faithing selves. And thus the question for a parent to ask is this: What is it to be Christian with my child? To seriously address that question is to discover what sort of environments, experiences, and interactions are necessary for our own and another's life in faith. To live with others in Christian ways, to put our words into deeds and our deeds into words, to share life with another, to be open to influence as well as to influence, and to interact with other faithing selves in a community of Christian faith is to provide the necessary environment for experienced faith.

AFFILIATIVE FAITH

If the needs of experienced faith have been adequately met during the childhood and early adolescent years, persons may begin to adopt an affiliative style of faith. During this period persons seek to act with others in an accepting community with a clear sense of identity. All of us need to feel that we *belong* to a self-conscious community and that through our active participation can make a contribution to its life. Persons with affiliative faith need to participate in the community's activities—for example, serving at a fellowship supper, singing in the choir, having a part in the Christmas pageant, participating in a service project, belonging to a group in the church where they know everyone's name and they are missed when absent. Of crucial importance is the sense that we are wanted, needed, accepted, and important to the community. The character of our actions may change with age, but all of us need to feel that we belong to a community and have opportunities to act like someone who truly belongs.

I recall a young man describing this faith pilgrimage and explaining that one of his most significant experiences was in the year that he didn't go to church school but instead read comics, collected the offering, and maintained the attendance records. Why was this experience so important? Because for the first time he felt that he belonged.

A second characteristic of affiliative faith is seen in the dominance of the religious *affections*. Some of us have forgotten or ignored the primal importance of the religion of the heart. We have become too concerned too early with the activities of thinking in Christian education, and we forget that the intuitional mode of consciousness is of equal importance with the intellectual. Indeed, in terms of faith, actions in the realm of the affections are prior to acts of thinking, which is why participation in the arts—drama, music, dance, sculpture, painting, and storytelling—are essential to faith. We need opportunities to act in ways that enhance the religious affections. Opportunities for experiencing awe, wonder, and mystery, as well as chances to sing, dance, paint, and act, are needed by us all. Events like the annual Christmas pageant are important. Far greater attention needs to be given to the religion of the heart and those actions that encourage the development of religious affections.

The third characteristic of affiliative faith is a sense of *authority*. What I mean by authority is a community's affirmation of a story and a way of life that judges and inspires its actions. I recall the many times our children told us that everyone else was doing something and we simply replied, "That's fine, but that is not the Westerhoff way." And then we would tell the story of how the Westerhoffs have acted through the years and why that way of life is important to us. Identity and authority go hand-in-hand.

The church must constantly be aware of its story and its way. We need to hear and tell that story, and we need to act so as to internalize it as our story. Child-centered and life-centered education have sometimes forgotten that the story or tradition is of central importance. While faith is first experienced enactively, it is next experienced in images or stories. Learning the community's story is, therefore, an essential for faith.

Throughout our lives, but particularly in the childhood and early adolescent years, we need to belong to and participate in an identity-conscious community of faith. We need to act in ways that nurture our religious affections. And we need to act to internalize, rehearse, and personally own the story which undergirds the community's faith.

SEARCHING FAITH

Providing that the needs of affiliative faith have been met some time during late adolescence, persons may expand into searching faith. Searching faith also has three characteristics. First, there is the action of *doubt* and/or *critical judgment*. Sometimes painful and sometimes celebrative, those with searching faith need to act over against the understanding of faith acquired earlier. We seem to know this, at least in terms of adolescent family behavior, but we have neglected it when considering faith. For example, my teenagers sometimes think I am quite stupid and misguided. And while that is not easy to live with, it is important for them to believe it in order to acquire their own identity. The same is true of faith. In order to move from an understanding of faith that belongs to the community to an understanding of faith that is our own, we need to doubt and question that faith. At this point the "religion of the head" becomes equally important with the "religion of the heart," and acts of the intellect, critical judgment, and inquiry into the meanings and purposes of the story and the ways by which the community of faith lives are essential. Serious study of the story and engagement with historical, theological, and moral thinking about life become important. The despairs and doubts of the searching soul need to be affirmed and persons need to join others in the intellectual quest for understanding.

A second characteristic of searching faith is *experimentation*. Searching faith requires that we explore alternatives to our earlier understandings and ways, for people need to test their own tradition by learning about others. It is only then that they are able to reach convictions which are truly their own.

And third, searching faith embodies the need to *commit* our lives to persons and causes. Persons with searching faith sometimes appear fickle, giving their lives to one ideology after another, sometimes in rapid succession and on occasion in contradiction.

But that is how we learn commitment. How can we know what it means to give our life away until we have learned how to do it? It appears, regretfully, that many adults in the church have never had the benefit of an environment which encouraged searching faith. And so they are often frightened or disturbed by adolescents who are struggling to enlarge their affiliative faith to include searching faith. Some persons are forced out of the church during this state and, sadly, some never return; others remain in searching faith for the rest of their lives. In any case, we must remember that persons with searching faith still need to have all the needs of experienced and dependent faith met, even though they may appear to have cast them aside. And surely they need to be encouraged to remain within the faith community during their intellectual struggle, experimentation, and first endeavors at commitment.

OWNED FAITH

Providing that the needs of searching faith have been met some time in early adulthood, we may expand into an owned style of faith. This movement from experienced and affiliative faith through searching faith to owned faith is what historically has been called *conversion*. Conversion experiences may be sudden or gradual, dramatic or undramatic, emotional or intellectual, but they always involve a major change in a person's thinking, feeling, and willing—in short, in their total behavior. Due to the serious struggle with doubt that precedes it, owned faith often appears as a great illumination or enlightenment, but in any case it can be witnessed in our actions and new needs. Now people most want to put their faith into personal and social action, and they are willing and able to stand up for what they believe, even against the community of their nurture.

Typically, persons owned by their faith strive to *witness* to that faith in both word and deed. They struggle to eliminate any dissonance between their faith as stated in their beliefs and their actions in the world. The words of St. John: "Whoever claims to be dwelling in Christ, binds himself to live as Christ lived" (I John 2:6), confront them with a new challenge. Persons with owned faith want and need the help and support of others in sustaining and in putting their faith to work. Of course, remember, the characteristics of searching faith are never eliminated, doubt and intellectual struggle continue but are dealt with in new ways. Still liberation, wholeness of life, spiritual health, and identity are known and persons can live a life in but not of the world. The radical demands of the Gospel can now be met.

Owned faith, personal identity, is God's intention for every person. To reach owned faith (our full potential) is a long pilgrimage in which we need to be provided with an environment and experiences that encourage us to act in ways that assist our expansion of faith. Let us never forget, however, that while the fulfillment of our potential ought to be the aim of all faithing selves, Christ died for us all, and no matter what style of faith we possess none are outside his redeeming grace.

We who are engaged in the church's educational ministry need to commit ourselves to helping each other fulfill our potential as corporate faithing selves, possessed by the Gospel and living according to its radical demands in the world. To do so we need to provide the experiences and environments which encourage those interactions necessary for the expansion of faith. However, it would be well to remember that these styles of faith are not to be used so much to design educational programs for others as to help each of us to understand our personal faith pilgrimage, establish our own needs, and seek interactive experiences with others so we might sustain and expand our own faith. Still, we need to realize that such efforts will contribute to the expansion of others' faith.

CONCLUSIONS

While these four styles of faith, characteristic of the faith pilgrimage of Christians, are important to understand if we are to take seriously enculturation as the means of Christian education, a few comments are in order before I proceed to discuss the implications of this understanding for the educational program of the church.

First, if we take seriously the styles of faith and faith's expansion, we must conclude that no single educational program for any age-group is valid. Consider adolescents in college (the group I know best). Some enter college ready to act with searching faith and we find them enrolled in college religion courses where the intellectual approach to the Bible and faith meets their needs. The chapel program with its experimental worship services, or even adventures into alternatives such as Zen Buddhist meditation, appeal to them. The college chaplain, who in the name of some ideology calls them to commitment, attracts their devotion and energy. However, there is another group of college students who have never had the needs of affiliative faith satisfactorily met and obviously are not found at the chapel or in religion courses. Instead, they are attracted to various Christian groups which emphasize belonging, the religion of the heart, and the authority of the story. These students will give hours to social service projects and they will talk about their beliefs, but little time is devoted to radical social action. Typically, they consider the religion faculty to be atheists and the chaplain in need of conversion. Conversion, in this case, is understood as the kind of dramatic, sudden, emotional experience many of them experienced as their transition into affiliative faith. We must not depreciate the importance of these students' faith pilgrimage, but rather we should celebrate their expanded faith and support them in their continuing quest.

We also need to be aware that few adults have owned faith, and that is why it is difficult to involve many adults in radical community and social action. Typically, adults have had their faith arrested in the affiliative style. In every church, therefore, a variety of educational environments and experiences that make possible the expansion of faith is needed. Remember, we can never offer a single educational program for all adults or all youth.

A second implication: While we need to provide experiences for each style of faith, we also need to provide experiences that help persons move from one style of faith to another. Such a movement is naturally made possible when life presents us with situations we cannot resolve satisfactorily through actions consistent with our present style of faith, and when we are presented with role models of persons acting more satisfactorily in an expanded style of faith.

Expansion of faith can also be aided or retarded by the community's rites of transition. Typically, for example, we have placed confirmation, which asks for a personal commitment of faith and a commitment to discipleship in the world, at the age when persons need to be encouraged to doubt, question, and experiment. The effect appears to be the arresting of faith. Perhaps confirmation should be moved to early adulthood and a new early adolescent rite celebrated on St. Thomas Day developed. This rite should encourage persons to make a covenant with God and the church and to struggle with their faith as Jacob wrestled with the angels.

If we were to take such insights seriously, we would involve ourselves and others in an educational ministry centered on experiences of interaction between and among persons according to their faith needs. For example, in the preschool and early childhood years we would encourage children to experience the word of God by interacting with those who are striving to be Christian with them through shared experiences. The rite of baptism could initiate persons into this style of faith, and prebaptismal preparation for expectant parents could enable them to act in ways helpful to those in experienced faith. First communion during first or second grade could initiate a person into affiliative faith. Intergenerational experiences (in a belonging community where the story is expressed, owned, and known) through participation in the arts could frame the church's educational ministry during the childhood and early adolescent years. The Sunday school (at least as it was understood in the nineteenth century) could provide a structure for such experiences between and among children, youth, and adults of all ages.

At some point in early adolescence we need a ritual to affirm persons in searching faith. As such, this ritual should encourage actions which emphasize the importance of intellectual inquiry and interpretation, bless the existential struggle with doubt, support experimentation with alternative understandings and ways, and facilitate commitment to persons and causes. Spiritual life retreats, short-term interest groups, small intensive study groups, and a variety of interactions in and outside the church between adolescents and adults with owned faith are needed to support searching faith. Confirmation is best saved for early adulthood. Extensive (one or two years) and intensive activities are needed to prepare persons for this important initiation into owned faith. Next come experiences and interactions based upon action-reflection or the implication of Christian faith for individual and social life. But more of this in the next chapter.

To conclude, when we make enculturation the means of Christian education, we turn to faith. That is, we consider its nature and character and the sorts of experiences and interactions, between and among persons within a community of faith, which encourage and support the expansion of faith. Specific activities and resources may not be easily identified, but at least we can be sure that we are struggling with the right questions. Namely: What is it to be Christian together? How can we live our individual and corporate lives under the judgment and inspiration of the Gospel to the end that God's community is come and God's will is done? What can I bring to share with another as a believer in Christ and a member of his church? What are Christian understandings and ways, and how can we express and experience them with others? How can we be open to one another so that as faithing selves in community we might all expand in our faith?

Answers to such questions will not be simple or easy, but they are at the heart of our educational mission and ministry, and they hold some vital resolutions as to whether or not our children will have faith.

UPDATE

My thinking as presented in this chapter has not radically changed, but I have added another way to understand this chapter's insights. There are three ways to understand the learning process in people. The first is in terms of chronological age; we speak of childhood, adolescence, and adulthood as times in the life cycle, and we speak of the aging process. In this view, one metaphor for curriculum is a production line. A learner or child is a valuable piece of raw material, a parent or teacher is a skilled technician, and the process is one of molding each piece of valuable raw material into the adult or teacher's design. We do things *to* people so as to aid their growth into adulthood. Such was the philosophy of John Locke and the behavioral psychology of B. E Skinner. In learning situations we categorize people by age. Children are typically seen as dependent, pre-rational, and nonproductive (they play). Adults are independent, rational, and productive. The adults, therefore, must do something to the children to make them into adults. There is some truth to this understanding, but it is limited.

The second understanding is in terms of developmental stage. We speak of human beings in terms of stages in human development and we speak of the maturation process from lower to higher stages of development. We categorize people by developmental, cognitive stages. Our curriculum metaphor now becomes a greenhouse. The child or student is a seed, the teacher or parent is a gardener, and the process is caring for these seeds until they grow up naturally. This is the philosophy of Rousseau and the developmental psychology of Piaget. Now we do things *for* people. There is truth in this understanding also, but it is limited.

The third understanding is in terms of characteristics of life. We speak of human beings as persons in relationships and we speak about the life process. Now we bring people together according to interest. In this view, our curriculum metaphor is a pilgrimage. A learner is a pilgrim, the teacher is a co-pilgrim, and the process is one of a shared journey together over time. We do things *with* people. It is this metaphor that provides us with a new way to understand people and learning. This is an alternative to the styles of faith I discussed in this chapter.

Using a pilgrimage metaphor for human life, I have named three distinct "pathways" to God. Each leads fully to God; none is superior to the others. While it is natural and wise for persons of all ages to begin with the first, each way may be traveled at any time, in any order, according to personal capability, interest, or need. Similarly, persons may return to traverse any trail at will, if the need or desire exists. Interestingly the third trail holds in creative tension the other two. In some cases our capabilities may limit us to one pathway, but if that occurs, nothing essential is lost. However, if we are able to travel all three paths and we choose not to do so, something in our lives is lost, for pilgrims are those who find meaning in the journey as much as in the journey's end.

The *first path* I have named the *experiential way*. On this slow, easy path people choose to participate in the life of a faith community, a family-like, caring, nurturing, intentional community, which retells and re-presents its sacred story, its memory and vision, through its cultic life. Within such a community the faith, people's character, consciousness, and interior life are formed. Along with others, people seek to focus on the intuitive way of thinking and knowing nurtured by participation in the arts and expressed through symbols, sacred stories, and rituals. On this pathway the authority of the community is assumed and trusted as persons engage in making the community's story their own and in establishing their identities as members of a story-formed community of faith.

The *second path* I have named the *reflective way*. On this difficult and sometimes painful traversing over the rocks, people need a community that will encourage and support them in being vulnerable to the search for meaning and purpose. On this pathway, people are encouraged to make sense of their lives in the light of their experience and the community's story. Concerned with believing and understanding, they engage in the necessary process of individuation and its concomitant process of searching for trustful intimacy with others. They are encouraged to assume responsibility for their own faith and life, and they quest after the intellectual knowledge that results from rational reflection on their experience and is expressed in terms of signs, concepts, and moral actions. The authority of community is tested as people seek both to internalize the community's tradition and to reshape it.

The *third path* I have named the *integrative way*. On this path the community encourages people to resolve any dissidence that may have been experienced by traversing the other two ways, by bringing them into creative tension or integration. Here, people are concerned with discerning; they therefore seek the help of the community in addressing the question, "How are we, as believers in Jesus Christ and members of his story-formed community, to live in community for the benefit of others and act as Christ's body in the world?" On this pathway, people combine both intuitive and intellectual ways of knowing and find meaning in both contemplation and action in a world understood as having two dimensions—the sacred (emphasizing the nonmaterial and pre-rational) and the secular (emphasizing the material and rational).

People seek to reconcile the paradox of Catholic substance (and its need to conserve the tradition) and a reformed spirit of prophetic judgment (and its need to retradition). No longer caught between believing either that there is "the truth," which only their authority knows and which must be blindly accepted, or that there is nothing but "relative truth," implying that every person is his or her own authority, they are now able to deal with pluralism's options. They can acknowledge, affirm, and advocate truth for their own lives while remaining open to others. Within a community of faith, people on this path live dependent upon God and interdependently with each other. In the words of T. S. Eliot, "We shall not cease from exploration and the end of all our exploring will be to arrive where we started and know the place for the first time."

Thus, those on the integrative path are able to affirm those traveling the other two paths. People on the other two paths help those on the third to maintain their integrative way. People on the experiential path keep those on the reflective from going too far afield; those on the reflective path keep those on the experiential path from not going far enough. Each, therefore, is in need of the others; each contributes to the life of the others. A healthy community of faith has people on all three paths, encouraging one another as they journey together in community. From the characteristics-of-life point of view, childhood encompasses the experiential way, adolescence the reflective way, and adulthood the integrative way.

CHAPTER FIVE

Hope for the Future

Christian education is to be thought of, through and through, as the Christian religion in operation.
George A. Coe

Assuming that the community of faith-enculturation paradigm provides us with a frame of reference which corresponds with our experience and is coherent with our theological assumptions, we still need to test it for practical relevance. A good theory is always usable. To be valuable, the community of faith-enculturation paradigm needs to aid us in planning and evaluating our church's educational ministry, and I find it does just that. During the last two years I have worked with a number of different local churches on various aspects of the paradigm's application. This final chapter will report a few representative examples.

EVALUATION AND PLANNING

The first use I will share involves educational planning in a United Church of Christ congregation in the South. To begin, they define their educational ministry: "Christian education is all the deliberate, systematic, and sustained efforts we make in any aspect of our parish life which enable us as persons and as a community of faith to be more Christian in our individual and corporate lives." They further defined Christian as "living under the judgment and inspiration of the Gospel to the end that God's will is done and God's community comes." And they agreed that their educational ministry is a lifelong process involving persons of all ages, not confined to the church school but including the total program of their church: (a) their ritual-ceremonial life; (b) the experiences persons have within their congregational life; and (c) their individual and corporate actions in society.

The church's educational ministry, they concluded, is to be judged by how well it (a) sustains and transmits the Christian faith tradition; (b) nurtures the expansion of faith and the spiritual lives of persons; and (c) equips and motivates the church and its members to fulfill their Christian vocation in the world.

Affirming the insights expressed in the last chapter on styles of faith and the expansion of faith through interactions in specific environments, the congregation formulated clearly stated and agreed-upon aims for their church's educational ministry under the headings of *Tradition, Persons,* and *Society.* Then, in terms of affiliative, searching, and owned styles of faith, they suggested in general terms what educational experiences needed to be provided. Their conclusions, which follow, are not offered because they are a perfect example to be copied, but because they demonstrate the practical usefulness of the community of faith-enculturation paradigm.

The Tradition

Aim one: To possess a personal knowledge and understanding of God's revelation as found in the Bible, and to be disposed and able to interpret its meaning for daily individual and social life.

To achieve this aim we need: (a) To be introduced to the biblical story of God's action in history (as found in the stories of the Old and New Testaments) as *our* story; (b) to be involved in an historical, critical interpretation of the biblical story; (c) to be engaged in reflection on current social issues in the light of the biblical story.

Aim two: To possess a personal knowledge and understanding of the Church's history and be disposed and able to interpret its relevance for daily individual and social life.

To achieve this aim we need: (a) To be introduced to the story of our foreparents' struggles to understand the faith and live faithfully in the world as *our* story; (b) to be involved in a critical historical investigation of the faithfulness of the institutional church throughout its history; (c) to be engaged in reflection on our contemporary striving to be a responsible and responsive community of faith in the light of our history.

Aim three: To possess a personal knowledge and understanding of the Christian faith as expressed historically in the church's creeds, cathechisms, and theological formulations; and to be disposed and able to reflect theologically on contemporary life and history.

To achieve this aim we need: (a) To be provided with experiences in community which are consistent with Christian understandings of God, persons, and society; (b) to be introduced to the historic attempts of the people of God to express their faith and to engage in a critical evaluation of our contemporary expressions of faith; (c) to be engaged in reflections on contemporary life in the light of the church's historical affirmations so as to aid us in expressing our faith in meaningful ways today.

Persons

Aim four: To be committed to Jesus Christ as Lord and Savior.

To achieve this aim we need: (a) To be introduced to a community of persons who live their lives as an expression of faith in Jesus Christ as Lord and Savior; (b) to be confronted with a clear intellectual understanding of the Gospel; (c) to be provided with opportunities for a personal decision for or against the affirmation that Jesus Christ is Lord and Savior.

Aim five: To possess a personal relationship with God in Christ and to be aware of God's continual revelation.

To achieve this aim we need: (a) To have our intuitional and historical modes of consciousness enhanced and be introduced to the life of a community of meditation, prayer, and worship; (b) to be aided in our struggles of the soul and be given opportunity to experiment with various forms of meditation, prayer, and worship; (c) to be provided with opportunities to identify God's actions in contemporary history and to celebrate meaningfully in community God's past and present actions in history.

Aim six: To be a faithful and responsible member of the Christian community of faith and to share in its life and mission.

To achieve this aim we need: (a) To be offered experiences which enhance our sense of belonging to a loving, caring, affirming community of faith; (b) to be aided in building a sense of trustful, responsible relationships with others and to be provided opportunities for service in the church's life and mission; (c) to be engaged in meaningful participation in the church's life, worship, fellowship, evangelism, stewardship, service, social action, and governance.

Society

Aim seven: To be aware of our Christian vocation and be able to make moral decisions in the light of the Christian faith and to be disposed to act faithfully and responsibly in daily individual and corporate life.

To achieve this aim we need: (a) to be provided with experiences foundational to moral decision-making, and be exposed to role models of the Christian life; (b) to be given opportunities to apply Christian faith to individual and social life; (c) to be enabled to act and reflect faithfully and responsibly in our individual and corporate lives, to the end that God's kingdom comes and God's will is done.

Aim eight: To understand and be committed to the church's corporate mission in the world for justice, liberation, whole community, peace, and the self-development of all peoples, and be disposed and able to engage in the continual reformation of church and society.

To achieve this aim we need: (a) to be introduced to a community of faith engaged in mission and be provided foundations for an awareness of corporate selfhood, justice, freedom, community, and peace; (b) to be given opportunity to commit one's life to social causes for the reformation of church and society; (c) to be equipped and motivated to engage in the reformation of the church and society on behalf of justice, liberation, whole community, peace, and the self-development of all people.

Aim nine: To possess an appreciative understanding of other faith traditions (Christian, Jewish, Muslim, Hindu, etc.) and to be able to enter into meaningful dialogue and action with them without sacrificing the integrity of one's own faith.

To achieve this aim we need: (a) To be exposed to persons of other faith traditions and their customs and ways; (b) to be helped to explore intellectually and experimentally the faith of other persons; (c) to be engaged in meaningful dialogue and actions with persons of other faiths.

HOLISTIC EDUCATION

My second illustration comes from a small United Methodist Church in the Southwest. Working from the community of faith-enculturation paradigm, they examined their situation and proposed a one-year education program to meet their needs. To accomplish this plan, the ministers and official board of the church went on a retreat where the first step was to write a two-page group description of their church and community:

Our church is situated in a small, expanding community. An increasing number of Roman Catholic Mexican-Americans have moved into the homes which surround our church; and as this has occurred, the congregation has tended to move farther and farther out from the city. As a result, active participation in the church's life and attendance at Sunday services has been negatively affected. Nevertheless, some 300 persons still consider this their church and no other churches exist at present in the emerging suburbs to which they have moved.

Our church is typical of many mainline churches in that it is characterized by its pluralism. There are both the more theologically and socially liberal and the more conservative. There are both the aging and the young, new people and old. Most of the members, however, are upper-middle-class white leaders in the community: bankers, storekeepers, business owners, ranchers, farm owners, doctors, lawyers, and teachers. The town's mayor, two members of the town council, three school board members, and the police chief are also church members. Our people are most concerned about the Mexican-Americans moving into the community, increasing taxes, and the changing character of this once quiet and secure community.

The church is quite traditional. It has all the committees churches usually have and a large number of organizations: three women's groups, one men's, one couples', two youth's (junior high and senior high). Membership in the youth groups has dwindled off to almost nothing and the parents are concerned. The couples' club is seen as the community's finest "social club," and many belong who do not belong to the church. The women's and men's groups, while primarily social in nature, are still active, live organizations that give significant amounts of time and money to the church.

The church is controlled by the older, long-time residents of the community, and new people have a hard time breaking into its leadership. The pastor emeritus, who had served the church for many years, lives in the community and is loved and respected. He has always had a strong social consciousness but was never able to move the church to action. The district superintendent also attends the church.

Attendance at Sunday services is decreasing. Whereas the older people want a traditional service, the new folk want something different. The church school attendance is also dwindling. Young families frequently go away on weekends, teachers are hard to secure, and children drop out early. No adult Sunday school exists at present.

Recently a crisis has occurred. The fire inspector declared the church school building, which is attached to the church, a fire hazard. A wealthy member is prepared to give a blank check to the church council for the building of a new church school in memory of his wife, who was the Sunday school superintendent for twenty-five years. Some of the members wonder whether anyone will ever use a new church school building, but there are some older members who believe that a new church school building would solve the church's problems.

There are a number of other things about this community that need to be known. A school bond issue for a new school and new education programs for the increasing number of Mexican-Americans is to be voted on in six months, and feelings are running high on this matter. To complicate matters, Caesar Chavez is said to be coming to organize the farm workers. People are talking about little else.

A number of new, younger families are very much concerned about changing the church's life and being more relevant to community issues. They are getting vocal, but they aren't represented on any official boards or committees. Most church members have a feeling something isn't right and they are beginning to hurt. Everyone seems to want some change, but most are looking backward for insight at present. There is a lot of confusion in people's minds about their faith and they are groping. They wish God was more real and life was more meaningful.

By the end of the weekend they had developed a five-part program for educational ministry during the following year. That was three years ago. I will describe each aspect of their approval and report the results.

Worship

Just prior to this planning meeting the bishops of the United Methodist Church issued a "Call for Peace and Justice Among All Peoples." They decided to make this call and its scriptural foundations the focus of their worship during the Lenten season. Each week a committee of two lay adults, a youth, the pastor, and the pastor emeritus would work together on the sermon. Each sermon (to be limited to ten minutes) was to take the shape of a dialogue between the pastor and the pastor emeritus. Following each dialogue sermon, the congregation was to be given ten minutes to respond. The sermon was to be set in the context of a modified Moravian love feast. That is, coffee and a sweet roll were to be served to each adult and juice and cookies to the children. The children were also given crayons and paper for use during this twenty-minute period. In the context of their sharing in a love feast, the sermon would be preached and responded to. Further the pastor and the pastor emeritus agreed to engage in an increased, systematic program of parish-calling in order to elicit feedback to their sermons. They hoped, through these means, to confront the congregation with the Gospel and its relevance for their social situation.

Church School

Since they did not have a building to meet in, they decided to meet in people's homes one evening each week in intergenerational neighborhood groups. They chose as their content a number of visionary passages from the Scriptures such as: "I will give you rain at the proper time; the land shall yield its produce and the trees of the countryside their fruit. Threshing shall last to vintage and vintage till sowing; you shall eat your fill and live secure in your land" (Lev. 26:4-6). "They shall beat their swords into mattocks and their spears into pruning knives; nation shall not lift up sword against nation nor ever again be trained for war" (Is. 2:4). "They shall know that I am the Lord when I break the bars of their yokes and rescue them from those who have enslaved them. I will give prosperity to their plantations; they shall never again be victims of famine in the land nor any longer bear the taunts of the nations" (Ez. 34:27, 29). "The arrogant of heart and mind he has put to rout, he has brought down monarchs from their thrones, but the humble have been lifted high. The hungry he has satisfied with good things, the rich he sent empty away" (Lk. 1:51-53). "Then I saw a new heaven and a new earth, for the first heaven and the first earth had vanished, and there was no longer any sea. I saw the holy city, new Jerusalem, coming down out of heaven from God, made ready like a bride adorned for her husband. I heard a loud voice proclaiming from the throne: 'Now at last God has his dwelling among persons! He will dwell among them and they shall be his people, and God himself will be with them. He will wipe away every tear from their eyes; there shall be an end to death, and to mourning and crying and pain; for the old order has passed away" (Rev. 21:1-4).

Each intergenerational neighborhood group was to explore the meaning of these passages and express them in music, dance, drama, or one of the plastic arts. Then once each month on a Sunday evening they gathered in the fellowship hall of the Roman Catholic Church (across the street from their church) to have supper together and share their creations.

Town Meetings

They decided to hold a series of town meetings to air the issues confronting the community and give the various sides an opportunity to share their views. They proposed that the district superintendent contact the Roman Catholic priests, the Jewish Rabbi, and the ministers of the six other Protestant churches to get their support. Their hope was to hold one town meeting at each church and to place these meetings in the context of worship.

Issue/Action Group

They voted to create a group to explore the school bond issue and engage the congregation in an effort to consider that issue in the light of the Gospel.

Future Planning

The man who offered to give the church a check for a new church school building was asked to chair a planning committee made up of one representative from each board and group in the church and an equal number of youth and adults not in leadership positions. They were to begin with Bible study on the church and its mission. Following that study, they were to create a five-year vision for their church. From that vision they were to formulate five-year goals. The next step was to consider events which, if they were occurring in two years, would make their five-year goals possible. These events were turned into objectives. Lastly, they were to design strategies and estimate costs for reaching these objectives. They were then to report their plans to the church and seek the support of the congregation.

Persons at the planning retreat were assigned to each of these five task forces and a means was developed to report their plan to the congregation and to secure the congregation's ownership.

When they returned they did just that. The church approved and they proceeded, with some unusual results. Attendance at worship increased. The people found they liked whole families worshiping together, and other changes began to occur in their worship life to make it more meaningful to all ages. The church school was reborn. They decided to continue the intergenerational church school, using the church lectionary as the content for their sessions and the arts as the basis of their activities. All but two Protestant churches cooperated in the town meetings. A new ecumenical spirit emerged, and while there was still much disagreement over community issues, they saved the community from being blown apart. Due in part to the "religious educational" efforts of the issue-action group, the bond issue passed.

The planning group proposed for the future: (a) family worship; (b) the renovation of the church (rather than the building of a new building); (c) the creation of an endowment for church mission and program; and (d) the continuation of an intergenerational church school. The renovation plans were quite radical. They voted to take the pews out of the church and turn the nave into an all-purpose room for education, worship, and fellowship, with rugs on the floor and an adjoining kitchen and library meeting room. The basement was turned into a day care center for the community, church offices, and storage. The intergenerational church school was moved from homes to the church and was held on Sunday evenings in the context of celebration, learning, and fellowship. Worship for all ages continued in the morning. The day care center became an ecumenical venture open to the community. The church raised funds for the renovation and the chairperson of the planning group created an endowment to support the day care center and other church programs.

In the process they lost fifty-two members (many of them the older, more affluent members). They also gained twenty-eight new members (a net loss of twenty-four), but they increased pledges so that the church was more financially secure than before. More important, the church had come to life.

A NEW CHURCH SCHOOL FOR DEPENDENT FAITH

The descriptions that follow are of a variety of educational programs that are consistent with the community of faith-enculturation paradigm. Each is an example of a reformed church school. They may or may not meet on Sundays, and they may or may not meet every week. When they do meet, they bring together children, youth, and adults for common activities. Music, dance, drama, the plastic arts, and filmmaking provide the dominant forms of expression. Integral to their life is celebration; the focus of programs is the Christian story, and the primary concern is for opportunities to be Christian together.

The following examples are based upon actual churches, all under 300 members, of several denominations, and without employed professional educators. The first is a small New England congregation. At a church meeting each year the people decide on a series of themes for their Sunday school. Last year they chose Moses and the Exodus, Advent-Christmas, Contemporary Christians, and Life in the Early Church. The Sunday school meets intergenerationally for four blocks of time during the year, and each thematic unit is assigned to a group of families who create and lead the Sunday school for that period. The first block of time runs from the first day of school through Thanksgiving. During the summer those who are interested prepared a dramatization of episodes in Moses' life. In the first week they presented a dramatization; the next week interest groups were formed.

There was an opportunity to make unleavened bread, and to create poetry of modern parallels to Moses' experience—and an art group illustrated the poetry. Other activities were taken from *The Jewish Catalogue,* one of the truly great resources needed for the Sunday school of the future. There was even a group who used the dark, dirt-filled, junk-strewn basement of the church to create a simulation of the Israelites' faith during the darkness of the long exodus. Two weeks of these activities led to two weeks of planning for a Seder, using Waskow's *Freedom Seder* as the basis for their celebration. Then came two weeks of preparation for a special Thanksgiving celebration, where there was an opportunity to identify the Congregational Puritan history with the Exodus. The unit ended with a grand Thanksgiving celebration, at which five grains of corn were put at everyone's place, a child asked why, and the story was told of the year when that was all their foreparents had for which to give thanks. After a few weeks people were ready to begin the Advent-Christmas theme.

Another example is a midwestern Sunday school that used the church lectionary to determine their Sunday school program, in which the Scripture lesson read in church each week would be used as the text for the sermon and the focus of the Sunday school hour. The week I observed, the lesson was Romans 5:20: "Moreover the law entered, that the offense might abound. But where sin abounded, grace did much more abound." The theme was "You are Accepted." In this church, people twelve years and older volunteer to be responsible for organizing diverse activities around the theme. They gather during the previous week for planning.

On this particular week, after they sang some hymns and folk songs, the lesson for the day was read and various activities were announced. One teen-age girl said that she wanted to talk about acceptance and paint pictures, and a group of ten gathered around a table she had set up in the hall. They talked about those in the community who were not accepted, and she commented that the Christian church accepts everyone, even if they don't deserve it. Then she suggested they all paint pictures. Most drew Indians, representing those not accepted, but one boy drew a tremendous monster urinating. The girl, in a validating manner, praised all the pictures and put them up on the wall. I watched the boy's face and saw it light up. I suspect that he had set out to test her statement that the Christian church accepts everyone, and as a result of her marvelously gracious act he had experienced grace.

In the same church that week, another scene was taking place in which one little boy spent the entire time destroying other people's work. No one felt that the situation was handled very well. During the break between Sunday school and family worship, the leaders for the week gathered to reflect on their experiences while the rest of the congregation engaged in fellowship and recreation. On this day the boy was the focus of concern. One of the adults asked if anyone knew what might be the matter. "Sure," said a teen-ager. "He wants attention." Well, what were they going to do about that? "Let's divide him up," one junior high girl suggested. "That is," she explained, "let's each take him for a week and be his special friend and give him all the attention he needs." They did, and that young boy also experienced grace. It would not be too dramatic to say that some day, when recalling his memories of the Sunday school, he will tell about this experience.

Another example is a West Coast church whose Christian education committee decided that it wanted to give a rebirth to the Sunday school. They were tired of cajoling people to teach and they were disturbed that children had stopped coming, so they scrapped the curriculum and decided to focus on drama, art, and music. Someone remembered reading about the old medieval plays that used to enact principal episodes from the Old Testaments. In medieval times the plays were undertaken by the craft guilds, analogous to our present-day trade unions, and when possible, the guilds presented plays that dealt with themes associated with their craft: the bakers presented the Last Supper, the goldsmiths the Adoration of the Magi, the shipwrights the Noah play, and so on. All the actors were amateurs, and scripts were usually superfluous because most of the players were illiterate. This church had families sign up in groups according to their favorite pastimes. There were such groups as mountain climbers, sailors, gourmet cooks, and musicians. Each group was given a biblical episode and told to create two dramas, one of the biblical story and one a contemporary expression of the story. Planning the drama was to be half the fun, and everyone was to have a part. There were costumes and props to be made and parts to be learned. Then during Lent everyone gathered and each group presented its play and involved everyone in it. This was followed by discussion and refreshments. The plays went so well that they decided to do it again the following year.

Another Southern church I'd like to mention chose the church year as its organizing principle. Activities were to be created which would help the congregation prepare for each season of the church year, and a season was assigned to existing groups and organizations in the church. The youth group was responsible for Pentecost, so they created an interesting group of activities for the weeks before Pentecost, and every child, youth, and adult chose a group to participate in. One group planned to bake and decorate a mammoth birthday cake for the church; another made banners for a parade symbolizing the works of the Holy Spirit; another made ceramic medallions to be given to those persons who renewed their confirmation vows at the Pentecost celebration. Other groups worked on original vocal and instrumental music, on a dramatic production of the account of Pentecost in Acts, and a last group designed and planned games from around the world for the church's birthday party. On Pentecost they united their labors for a fantastic celebration.

RELIGION OF THE HEAD
FOR SEARCHING FAITH

One day a minister posted a large advertisement on the church bul-
letin board. It read: "Wanted—Film Makers." "Subject: This church
vs. The Gospel." A group of eight persons gathered at the appointed
time and spent their first two meetings viewing short films, experimenting with a Super-8 projector, a previewer, an editing machine,
and discussing the hows of film-making. They decided their first
task was to understand the Gospel, since that was integral to the
concept of the film. Ten weeks were spent in concentrated study of
the synoptic Gospels, using the tools of biblical scholarship. At the
same time they shot as much footage of church life as they could
afford, and at the end of the eight weeks they began the process
of putting together their film. Another six weeks and they had a
film and tape entitled "The Judgment," which was then shown at a
church supper and followed by a discussion. As a result, a new four-
week seminar on the synoptic Gospels was led by the film-makers.

Another group used the *Learning To Be Free* resource, which I
developed with Joe Williamson and a group of young people from
a Congregational Church in Massachusetts (part of the United
Church of Christ's Shalom Curriculum). In this resource is a paper-
back, *Liberation Letters,* that contains a series of five letters I had
written to youth from various places around the world. This church
sent a copy of Liberation Letters to each eleventh- and twelfth-
grader, including those who hadn't been seen in some time. In the
book was a postcard to be returned to the church if they were interested in joining a group to work on liberation from a Christian
perspective. Those who returned the card were notified of a place
and time to meet, and copies of a process workbook, developed and
tested by the youth in Massachusetts, were made available.

The process developed like this: They worked at building a
learning, witnessing, faith community, and they explored the

Christian understanding of liberation. Then they identified where
they experienced oppression. (In their case they concluded that
they were oppressed by their public school library because it contained only books from a single perspective; that is, there was
no Malcolm X and no Karl Marx.) They developed a strategy in
which they asked the church for funds for books. No one asked
what books, but they were given a hundred dollars with which they
bought the books they felt were missing and presented them to the
school librarian. Troubled by the titles, she turned them over to
the principal, who passed them on to the superintendent. Soon the
school board had a decision to make and the whole community was
involved. When word got back to the church there were a number
of upset adults. As part of their strategy the youth had anticipated
trouble and had planned a series of meetings to aid the church in
looking at this issue in the light of the Scriptures, the church's history, and its theological affirmations. After six weeks of struggling
with the issue, the public school decided to accept approximately
one-third of the books, and the church voted to put the others in its
library.

Another example is found in a church that decided to build
serious study into all its boards and committee meetings as well
as other church gatherings. One evening the youth and adult choirs
had gathered to plan a "hymn sing" for Lent. They began by
making large name tags which also included each person's belief
about the relationship between Jesus and God. Next they went
around the room looking for those with whom they agreed. After
forming groups, each group was to find a hymn which expressed
their beliefs and write it on newsprint.

Following this exercise they saw the United Church of Christ
filmstrip, "The Council of Nicaea," and then discussed the Nicene
creed and summarized its contents: Christ is God; Christ is man;
Christ is one. Then they reviewed the beliefs expressed in their
hymns to make sure that each of these theological statements was

present and a balanced orthodox understanding of Jesus Christ was affirmed. Putting the hymns in the order to be sung, they also wrote up short histories of each hymn and a summary statement of its theological affirmation. Not only had they created an exciting hymn sing in the three hours, but they had learned much about Christian theology.

One last example is based upon a series of two-day spiritual life retreats that brought together a number of events and made possible an unusually "concentrated" educational experience. There were experiments in worship following the monastic hours, silence and meditation, critical Bible study, sharing of theological doubts and questions, exploration of other religions and their cultic life, discussions on commitment and the Christian life fellowship. Persons committed themselves to three of these retreats during the year, and after the third one they were responsible for sharing their struggles of the soul, intellectual quests, insights, and resolutions with the congregation.

Through these concentrated educational experiences in which some of the needs of searching faith—intellectual inquiry, action, and experimentation in community—are met, persons can be nurtured in the expansion of their faith.

WITNESS-ACTION EDUCATION FOR OWNED FAITH

One of the problems inherent in learning to apply our faith to life situations is the context in which we do our learning. You can teach a course in business ethics, but that does not mean people can or will use their learning when confronted by ethical issues in their office. People best learn to apply faith to life when they learn to do it in the context of their decision-making, a fact that I discovered in a fascinating way.

One day I was about to enter the hospital room of a parishioner and I met her doctor, another parishioner. He exclaimed, "My medical oath doesn't make sense anymore. I have kept Mrs. X alive in a vegetable state at a cost no one can afford for six months, and I can continue to do so. The question now is: ought I continue? And no one is helping me to solve that question." With that, he ran off and I went in to see Mrs. X. That night I went to see him and asked if other doctors were asking such questions, and if they ever discussed them. The result was a weekly two-hour luncheon, at a reserved table in the doctor's dining room of the hospital, in which we began each session with a case study of a patient that presented a moral dilemma. Then we sought to find solutions that were consistent with Christian faith.

From this experience I developed a number of principles for adult religious education: (1) Go where they are. Don't bring them to the church but engage in education in the midst of where they make their decisions and act. (2) Have a homogeneous group, not everyone alike, but people with the same questions, problems, and needs. (3) Never ask for more than five weeks' commitment. (4) Begin where they are, with their problems. (5) Work toward some action.

Through the years, these principles have proven particularly valuable for persons who are struggling to put their faith into action in the world. I have had experiences with groups of educators, lawyers, doctors, and government officials. One group which worked particularly well involved New York business people who had an hour-and-twenty-minute commute on a train each morning and night. In twenty minutes they read the *New York Times* and the *Wall Street Journal* and then they slept. So we rented one of the railroad cars. They all read their papers and then we had an hour to discuss business case studies. When we got to New York, I could experience their life, see them in action, and develop new cases to be addressed.

CONCLUSIONS

Examples could go on and on. Over the past two years I have found the community of faith-enculturation paradigm relevant, in practice, and indeed valuable as a theoretical frame of reference for reforming the church's educational ministry. Of course, a great deal more work needs to be done on the paradigm itself, as well as on its application. In this short tract I have only sought to introduce some preliminary conclusions that have been developing for a few years, but that needed to be expressed. Now the critical help of all those people in local churches who share my concern for the church's educational mission and ministry is needed. Together, revisions, clarifications, and expansions can be made. I suspect that we will make some mistakes, but future generations, aware of our shortcomings, surely will reform religious education once again. I hope to live long enough to support those reforms, for I have no desire to hold on to the present as the final word. Rather, my only wish is to be faithful to the Gospel and the needs of our day. That, I have striven to do. While time will reveal how successful I have been, I do believe that the community of faith-enculturation paradigm provides, for today, a frame of reference and an understanding of religious education that adequately and imaginatively addresses the question: Will our children have faith? Further, I believe it suggests ways to engage in religious education that can insure a positive response to that question. Our children will have faith if we have faith and are faithful. Both we and our children will have Christian faith if we join with others in a worshiping, learning, witnessing Christian community of faith. To evolve this sort of community where persons strive to be Christian together is the challenge of Christian education in the years ahead.

UPDATE

Churches go about planning in numerous ways. There is annual planning, in which a group gathers to plan for the next year as if it were simply an extension of the present year. In demand planning, the planning group responds to people's current demands, attempting to satisfy their desires. Crisis planning responds to the present crisis and then moves to the next. Utopian planning looks at churches that are being praised and attempts to copy their efforts. Problem-centered planning works to resolve or establish current problems. None of these means for planning ever breaks free of the present. Only vision planning can do that. Vision planning begins not with the present but with an imagined future and then returns to the present to decide what can be done now that will influence that potential future.

To engage in visionary planning is to be an intentional community of Christian faith and life. Four components should be considered.

- A consideration of the dimensions of our common life: the liturgical, ethical, spiritual, pastoral, and ecumenical (evangelism, mission, outreach, and stewardship) in a community of faith (see chapter three).

- A visionary understanding of the church as a community of faith as well as the process of formation, education, and instructional/training.

- A visionary understanding of the church's mission to be the Body of Christ in the world and clear catechetical aims.

- An accurate understanding of the congregation's context— historical, social, and cultural—as well as the congregation's own history, culture, denominational ethos, personality, and resources.

Afterword

As I explained in the Preface, *Will Our Children Have Faith?* was published in 1976. It was intended to be solely a "tract for our times," but whether our children will have faith is still the question about which I worry. It is a question that implies looking at many factors: the historical, social, and cultural context in which we live; our understanding of the Christian life of faith; our understanding of how persons acquire their world views, values, and lifestyles; and our ability to be the sort of community that can nurture and nourish such understandings.

HISTORICAL REFLECTIONS

Will Our Children Have Faith? begins with a chapter entitled "The Shaking of the Foundations." In it, I maintained the position that the discipline of Christian education, dominated by what I characterized as a "schooling-instructional" paradigm, placed the very foundations of educational theory and practice in question. Stated in a youthful, extremist, overly dramatic manner, this position was popular with lay critics but not with professional educators. Schooling and instruction had its defenders and rightly so, but I sensed anomalies in the paradigm that had dominated, without criticism, the discipline of Christian education for many years. Further, I expressed my conviction that because socialization processes had been largely ignored, we were unaware of the hidden curriculum that dominated our efforts, namely, that our educational programs were aimed at institutional incorporation rather than at the mature Christian life of faith.

A second chapter, entitled "Beginning and Ending with Faith," follows. In it, I boldly suggested that liberation theology provided Christian education with its most relevant theological system for establishing catechetical aims and means.

Over the years I have become clearer as to the nature and character of Christian community and the Christian life of faith, but I continue to defend the position I first presented in chapter two— that a "community of faith-enculturation" paradigm offers the most helpful way of perceiving catechesis in our day.

The third chapter is entitled, therefore, "In Search of Community." Here I made a first attempt to describe what an intentional community of faith might look like, a theme I took up again in a later book, *Living the Faith in Community*. At this point, however, my emphasis was on the importance of focusing our understanding of education on every aspect of congregational life—every action encouraged and every experience offered to children, youth, and adults, especially liturgy. Today I worry that the home and the parish as intentional communities of faith may not be adequate to the task and that a new radical understanding of parochial schools may be needed.

"Life Together" is the fourth chapter, and in it I made my first attempt to describe my understanding of the catechetical process as well as to say something about developmental theory and its relationship to the life of faith. It was also my first attempt to distance myself from the faith-development paradigm with its cognitive understanding of faith and its preferential higher stages. Instead I spoke of styles of faith and used the metaphor of rings on a tree as a way to show appreciation for its insights. I have come a long way since then and now speak of pathways to the spiritual life, but I still find this early attempt popular and helpful for many.

I closed with a chapter entitled "Hope for the Future" in which I told stories of congregations who in various ways were bringing my community of faith-enculturation paradigm into life through practical and relevant efforts to equip and encourage persons for the Christian life of faith. Since then I have moved from metaphors to concepts, from practice to theory. And now I strive to move from conceptual theory back to practical application.

As I reread this book, I became aware of its significance in shaping the emerging foundations for all of my work since. I also became painfully aware of its inadequacies. And so, in this short essay, I intend to return to some of the themes that emerged in *Will Our Children Have Faith?* and share my current understandings. I will do that by beginning where I began then, with an attempt to understand the context in which we live and its implications for our catechetical ministry.

THE BIRTH OF A NEW ERA

It has become increasingly clear to me that modernity is drawing to a close and a new historical, social, and cultural context is emerging. We live in a liminal period between the ending of one era and the birth of another. If a faithful catechetical ministry is to take shape, we must attempt to understand this emerging context.

I believe that one day historians will consider the twentieth century to be similar to the first, fourth, tenth, and sixteenth centuries. With the collapse of the medieval synthesis, modernity was born in the sixteenth century. The sixteenth century witnessed a reformation and a counter-reformation, a religio-political dislocation and a division within Western Christendom. With the seventeenth-century Renaissance came humanism, individualism, and scientific objectivism. The eighteenth-century enlightenment, with its focus on reason, was followed by a nineteenth-century romantic movement. The twentieth century is the era of technology in which the moral limits of modernity have begun to surface and a new era has begun to emerge.

In just such a time, revitalization movements emerge as attempts to reestablish the past as we have known it, while other movements engage in the difficult and sometimes painful task of moving into an unknown future without losing the benefits of the past. If we are to move into the future faithfully, it will be necessary to describe some of the historical, social, and cultural characteristics of modernity both in terms of its contributions and its limitations.

Modernity placed an unprecedented emphasis on the intellectual way of thinking and knowing. By doing so, it depreciated the intuitive way of thinking and knowing. Science replaced the arts and humanities in importance; confidence in instruction and schooling replaced a dependence on enculturalization. A countermovement among some Christians resulted in anti-intellectualism and indoctrination.

Modernity wisely sought to eliminate dualisms, such as being and doing and material and spiritual reality. One negative consequence was the emergence of a series of monisms: secularism, rationalism, and materialism. Because modernity was unable to imagine a spiritual reality that had both a material and nonmaterial dimension, a spiritual understanding of life lost relevance. At the same time, some Christians maintained the dualism of material and spiritual life that tended to manifest itself as a split between belief and daily life. Further, romanticism's attempt to reestablish a place for emotion resulted negatively in a split between thinking and feeling. This manifested itself in the church as pietism.

Functionalism also emerged, depreciating being and establishing doing as the sole definition of who we are. And where being and doing were held together, it was doing that defined being, rather than being that defined doing. Progress, making a difference, and being effective became important concerns. Attempts to build God's reign became common, although unsuccessful. For many, God was no longer present and active in human life and history. The question became "What should we do?" rather than "What is God doing with which we might cooperate?" Contemplative life was depreciated, and the active life assumed greater importance. For those Christians who were troubled by this position, God remained a deity who controlled all of life and who, on invitation, might break in to miraculously change the natural course of events.

In the course of modernity's development, all of life, including people, became objects for our investigation and manipulation. Life became a problem to be solved by autonomous individuals, through knowledge acquired by analytical reason, disinterested judgment, rational discourse, and decisions of the will. Natural theology and natural-law theory with its belief in a reasonable, cause-and-effect universe dominated our theological and moral thought. Even the Scriptures became an object for our study. Fundamentalism and biblical literalism emerged among those who were unhappy with modernity's historical-critical methodologies.

Lastly, during this male-dominated period, we became increasingly convinced that nature and history, society with its political and economic systems, and our own personal lives are manageable. At present, we believe either that we can be and ought to be in control of life and our lives or that we are victims of our heredity and environment. We appear to move between being totally independent or pathologically codependent. Any sense of being interdependent, communal beings fully dependent upon God, with whom all things are possible, appears to elude us. Christian education, which for centuries has accepted modernity's understanding and ways, must make major adjustment in terms of both catechetical ends and means.

These historical characteristics that are changing are

accompanied by major societal change, the third since the birth of the church. During the apostolic period (the first through the fourth centuries), the church existed in a hostile, alien environment in which being in but not of the world made sense. Tight boundaries and the conversion of adults seemed natural.

Then in the fourth century, Western Christendom was born. The church now found itself in a congenial environment. Boundaries weakened. There was little difference between being a Christian and being a good citizen, and the church's missionary efforts were directed to the heathen, pagan world. Sectarian movements emerged, but Christianity in general merged civil and religious life.

While some would strive to recreate this relationship, most admit that we must learn to live in a post-Christian society in which religion is not taken seriously in the public arena, in which religion is privatized, ignored, and trivialized by many. No longer can we assume that we live in a Judeo-Christian society. No longer can we assume that the public schools are friendly to or support Judeo-Christian values. No longer can we assume that we share a common language for engaging in moral discourse. Once again, the conversion of adults and a missionary movement at home are reasonable. The church's withdrawal from the world is for most unacceptable, but we cannot be sure what the future holds for the church. Of one thing we do seem to be sure: our assumptions about being citizens of the United States, as well as believers in Jesus Christ and members of his church, are changing radically. A new look at reformed parochial schools, the adult catechumenate and believers' baptism, and a renewed emphasis on adult catechesis are signs of the times.

A major cultural change is also occurring. Race as a biological category of social significance is found to be increasingly useless. Indeed, modernity's attempt to turn race into an important category resulted in the extremely negative effects of racism. Ethnicity, with its focus on groups with a common identity and heritage, has become more important. So has culture, that is, a people's learned, shared understandings and ways of life. Ethnicity and culture sometimes overlap, but the culture of the rich and the poor, the literate and illiterate, the city and the country, the North and the South differentiate persons within any single ethnic group.

Modernity tended to focus on division by race and the superiority of the white race. It also depreciated ethnicity and culture and focused its attention on the idea of a melting pot that would blend together all ethnic and cultural groups into a common American culture. Slowly, racial prejudice and uniculturalism have become unacceptable.

A new emphasis is being placed on the value of diversity. Such a pluralistic society assumes identity-conscious groups who are open to each other without relativizing differences and who are willing to engage in the difficult task of living together and striving for justice and peace. Aware of the complexities of this cross-cultural life, many would prefer to reaffirm uniculturalism or to work toward a multicultural society in which there is a distinct separation of divergent identity-conscious groups, which come together only when it is mutually beneficial.

Affirming in principle racial, ethnic, and cultural pluralism implies the difficult task of honoring diversity in worship, teaching, learning, common life, and proclamation of the Gospel, and yet maintaining a sense of unity and common mind.

More serious is the shift from a triumphalist understanding of Christianity's uniqueness to an affirmation of religious pluralism in principle as well as fact—a phenomenon that has led to the relativization and privatization of all religion. It is not yet clear what a society that accepts religious pluralism as reality but does not accept religious pluralism in principle will look like, but it will surely challenge the imagination of catechists.

THE CHALLENGE OF MAKING CHRISTIANS IN OUR DAY

Christianity is a way of life that emerges from a particular perception of life in general and in our own lives in particular. It is the life
of the baptized. "Christians," wrote Tertullian, the third-century
theologian, "are made [fashioned or formed], not born." The question then, as now, is how? For those in Tertullian's day the answer
was "catechesis" in Greek or "christening" in English. Catechesis
literally means to echo. In terms of the early church, it meant to
echo the Word—Jesus—that is, to make Christ-like communities
and persons. The church in every era has had to develop an understanding of this process in terms of its historical, societal, and cultural context. Living within a transitional era makes this task more
challenging.

But first it is important to acknowledge that the determinative
language of making, shaping, and forming Christ-like people is
unacceptable. We can indoctrinate, that is, do things to people in
an attempt to make them into our predetermined design, but that is
both morally and practically questionable. From a theological perspective, each person is a soul or self, an integrated being composed
of body, mind, and spirit, that freely interacts with the influences
of heredity and environment. No person's life is completely determined by internal or external influences. Jesus as savior has freed
humanity for responsible life. At the same time, such influences
have significant power and ought not to be discounted.

God, I suggest, will not judge either parents or the adult community on how their children turn out, but God will judge the
adults in the church on how they turn out, and that is enough for all
to lose sleep over. The issue is not what we have done to or for our
children in an attempt to make them turn out as we see fit, but what
we have done faithfully *with* our children in an attempt to influence their understandings and ways of life.

All of this becomes extremely complicated in a diverse culture such as ours, in which influences come from so many varied relationships: home and family, school, religious community, peer group (friends), voluntary associations (clubs, groups, and teams), and mass media.

Further, to be faithful to our historical, social, and cultural context, catechesis will need (1) to reaffirm the intuitive way of thinking and knowing, that is, to reaffirm the foundational roles of nature, the arts, and ritual in the lives of people; (2) to understand all of life as spiritual with two dimensions: one material, one non-material; (3) to affirm that being and doing are one, but that doing proceeds from being; (4) to perceive all of life as a subject that engages us rather than as an object for our manipulation; thus, we return to the praying of Scripture as a complement to the study of Scripture; (5) to acknowledge that nature, history, society, and our personal lives are unmanageable and that we are communal beings dependent upon a God who is present and active in human life and history, a God with whom we can cooperate; (6) to acknowledge further that life is best understood as mystery and ordered freedom in which we are bound by relationships that make influence possible but not determinative; and (7) to know that there is only one end of human life (all else being means)—to live in an ever-deepening and loving relationship with God, to live a life that manifests itself in an ever-deepening and loving relationship with one's true self (the self in the image of God), with all people, and with the natural world.

More difficult to determine is how to live faithfully as resident aliens in a post-Christian era. We will need to find a new way of being-in-but-not-of-the-world while we avoid being-in-and-of-the-world. How we decide this issue will affect not only the church's missionary presence in the world but also its catechetical ministry.

And if this does not complicate our situation enough, let us not forget our theological mandate to affirm in principle and practice racial, ethnic, and cultural pluralism, while maintaining the unity of a diverse community with a common mind, heart, and will.

Even still, all of this might be easy to accomplish except for the fact that there is no agreed-upon understanding of life and way of living among those who claim to be Christians. Until we can agree upon what a Christian looks like and can provide significant, contextually relevant, intentional, and foundational influences that have the potential of being formative in a healthy way, there is no reason to believe that the church can develop a faithful catechetical ministry. This challenge is even greater than dealing creatively with a postmodern world.

ACHIEVING CLARITY ON OUR CATECHETICAL AIM

Until we have some sense of what a Christian looks like, our efforts at catechesis will be irrelevant. As a first step to this end, we will need to rethink some of our general understanding. For example, during modernity, faith was understood as a cognitive term, as doctrine or the rational acceptance of prepositional statements about truth. Ethics focused on rational moral decision making. And the concept of consciousness was replaced by a concern for rational reflection on experience.

As a consequence, Christian education focused on instructional methods with which people could be taught what Christians believe, how to make a moral decision, and how to acquire rational insights by reflecting upon experience. However, as important as these ends might be, they are secondary when considering the Christian life of faith. Faith, while having an intellectual component of believing and discerning and an emotional component of worshiping and obeying, is essentially a matter of perception, a way of seeing and thereby comprehending life and our lives. Faith is given and a gift.

Faith cannot be arrived at through rational reflection or logical argument. While faith does not grow or develop, we can grow in faith.

Ethics is first of all concerned with character, that is, our sense of identity and how we are naturally disposed to behave. Only if we have Christian character will knowing how to make moral decisions have usefulness. We now realize that the value of being able to reflect upon experience is totally dependent upon consciousness, that is, our subjective awareness that makes it possible and reasonable to reflect upon particular experiences, such as the presence and action of God in our lives. Christian faith, character, and consciousness cannot be acquired through instruction, but can be made possible through other catechetical processes.

A Christian has a peculiar faith or perception of life and his or her life, a peculiar sense of identity and behavioral dispositions, and a peculiar consciousness. At baptism we are incorporated into Christ's body—the church. We are infused with Christ's faith, character, and consciousness and empowered to be Christ's presence in the world.

To be baptized is to share a common life of faith, a Christlike character and consciousness, a life intended to be radically different from the unbaptized. This life is a sign and a witness to an alternative way of living made possible by the life, death, and resurrection of Jesus Christ. God's desire for justice and reconciliation is realized through the continuing action of the Holy Spirit on all who perceive and accept Jesus as their savior and who, with God's help, abide in God's reign—that condition in which God's will is known and done.

As Christians, we are called to continue in the apostles' teaching and fellowship, the breaking of bread, and in prayer. We are called to persevere in resisting evil. Whenever we fall into sin, we are called to repent and return to the Lord. We are called to proclaim by word and example the good news that God's reign is within and among us. We are called to seek and serve Christ in all persons, loving our neighbors as ourselves. Finally, we are called to strive for justice and peace among all people, respecting the dignity of every human being.

Our characters will manifest the blessed, joyful, happy life Jesus described in the Beatitudes. We will be a people who acknowledge our helplessness and put our trust in God's grace—God's unmerited, loving presence and action in our lives. And being totally dependent on God, we will be a people able both to discern and to do God's will. Our tears will never end for the injustice, oppression, and suffering in the world even as we remorsefully acknowledge our participation in their causes. As a people who experience God's forgiving, transforming love we will be empowered to join God in striving for justice and peace.

Knowing our lives as unmanageable, we will turn them over to God. Realizing our ignorance and weakness without God, we will become examples of life as God intended it. Having hearts that strive for an ever-deepening and loving relationship with God, we will know and experience the true meaning, purpose, and end of human life.

Further, we will be a people who strive to make our motives as pure and holy as our actions. Thus, we will live self-critical lives ever striving, with God's help, to discern God's will. We will be a people who in our daily lives and work serve God by joining in God's ever-constant work of restoring all people to unity with God, with self, with all people, and with the natural world. We will, therefore, experience life as God intended it as sons and daughters, as brothers and sisters to each other. Finally, we will be a people willing to risk everything, including, if necessary, our own lives, to be Christ-like people, truly members of his body. We will be his presence in the world, abiding in God's reign until it comes in its fullness.

There is more, of course, but this peculiar composition of faith,

character, and consciousness is foundational to the life of the baptized and to the essential aims of catechesis.

UNDERSTANDING CATECHESIS

Catechesis, as I now understand it, is composed of three intentional, interrelated, life-long processes. I have named them formation, education, and instruction/training. The first is normative; the
second two are contributive.

Instruction/training is the means used to acquire the knowledge
and the skills foundational to the Christian life of faith, such as
knowledge of Scripture and the ability to interpret it. This process
is necessary, but it is not sufficient. Alone it could make possible a
person who knows all about Christianity and the Christian life but
has no desire to live it.

Education, as I use the word, is critical reflection on the Christian
faith and life in the light of Scripture, tradition, and reason, or it is
reflection on experience. This process is also necessary but not sufficient. Alone it could make possible a person with a fine critical
mind who is uncommitted.

Formation is an intentional effort to engage in enculturalization, the natural process by which culture, a people's understandings and ways of life, their world view (perceptions of reality), and
their ethos (values and ways of life) are transmitted from one generation to another.

Knowledge and skills are acquired through instruction and
training, the ability to reflect critically on every aspect of life in the
light of some standard is acquired through education, but a person's
faith, consciousness, and character are acquired through formation.
Formation, while foundational, normative, and necessary, is not
sufficient either. All three— formation, education, and instruction/
training—are essential for a faithful catechesis.

We could say that this model of catechesis is based upon how Jesus taught. Jesus went in search of students. His life was an example of what he proclaimed. Who he was and what he did were one. His way of life attracted followers whom he invited to identify with him, observe his way of life, and imitate him. As a foundation for his perceptions of life, he told stories, and he used parables to subvert the lives of his listeners so that they might creatively reflect on their faith and life. But mostly he invited people into a relationship with him and into a community of practice.

What I have named formation was central to how Jesus and the community that remained after Pentecost taught. Formation is best understood as the participation in and the practice of the Christian life of faith. It is a process of transformation and formation, of conversion and nurture. It is a natural process that is intentional. Others have been more concerned with instruction/training and education, but formation has been my passion and the dominant focus of my work for almost forty years.

When I first began to explore this natural process of enculturalization, I turned to cultural anthropology and its understanding of how cultural understandings and ways of life were transmitted from generation to generation. What I discovered were those dimensions of communal life that played a significant role in this process. The first and most important formative aspect of communal life is ritual participation, because its rituals encompass all the other formative aspects of its life. In this case, we are especially focused on its religious rituals or those repetitive symbolic acts (words and deeds) that express and manifest the community's sacred narrative.

Participation in the community's ritual life is followed by the environment in which communal life is experienced. This includes all that persons see, taste, touch, smell, and hear. The space we create has tremendous influence on us. Another formative influence is how the community orders time, and its calendar, through which it remembers significant historic events and people. Next is the community's organization of its life and how it encourages people to spend their time, energy, talents, and resources. This is followed by the ways people interact with and treat each other—how the community makes decisions, settles differences, and lives together. Another influence is established role models. Some are natural, such as parents and teachers, but others are those persons, past and present, whom the community establishes as examples to be emulated. Behavioral disciplines or activities encouraged and practiced regularly by the community are also important influences. And last is the influence of language, including vocabulary and grammar. The way the community names things and speaks about them influences our understandings and ways of life, our faith, characters, and consciousness.

CONCLUDING THOUGHTS

My thought continues to develop, and yet as I look back, I see an amazing amount of continuity over the years. I am challenged by George Lindbeck's contention in *The Nature of Doctrine* that Western culture is now in an intermediate stage in which effective enculturation is questionable and that the Christian church is in a liminal era in which faithful catechesis is impossible. He may be correct, but as a parish priest, I am committed to continue my quest for a faithful catechesis, while knowing there are no guarantees.

I remain convinced that the next generation may have faith but only if the present generation in the church is faithful in living that life of faith with them. And I trust they will. Why? Because I believe that God is present and active in human life and that the Holy Spirit will continue to inspire and empower a faithful remnant in the church.

A Memoir

Memoir is a French word with its Latin root in memory. Our memoirs are revealing and can be troubling. While it is difficult to remember every experience, the question remains why did we remember one experience and not another? What is it about our memories that makes us believe that some particular idea is ours, when in fact we borrowed it from someone one else? Memories are selective. They tell us more about the one who remembers than the reality upon which those memories are founded. There is always a reason for what we remember or forget, though it may not be known. Some of our memories are distortions of reality. Some are not only forgotten but rejected and even denied. We often laud the role of experience in our lives, but experiences need not only to be remembered, they also can require reflection and interpretation before their validity or meaning can be understood.

I typically explain to my students that I doubt that they will ever know or remember what I say. They will only know and remember what they choose to hear (the latter being more important for their learning), but only if they ask why they choose to hear and remember what they did. To aid them on this learning pilgrimage they need to take their own notes of what they believe important in what they heard, rather than try to take notes of what they may believe I said. Regretfully, in higher education the giving of lectures has been the dominant mode for teaching. Professors give lectures, student take notes, and exams test how well they heard what the professor said. Fortunately this mode of teaching is slowly changing.

Which is why I remember that over the years I have become far more interested in learning than teaching. Little by little I have shifted my emphasis from teaching to helping students to learn, from lectures to interactive learning in which every student can use their particular way of learning and contribute it to the efforts of others. Therefore, I have come to believe that teachers need to provide alternative ways of learning. For example, extroverts tend to need a small group with which to interact, but introverts need to go off to be alone in order to process what they have read or heard. Some learners can only learn by doing, by being involved in an activity that produces an experience and others learn best by being contemplative in processing experiences. One of my favorite exams asks students to name a present problem or question that now concerns them that they did not have when the course began and how they planned to discover an answer in the future.

A single question continues to haunt my memory. For more than fifty years (I was ordained in 1958) I have been on a pilgrimage to discover how congregations and persons become Christian. How can we be sure we know what a Christian looks like and how do we proceed in our particular time in history to make Christ-like communities and persons? In this memoir I want to share with you the memories of my continuing quest to answer these questions, inviting you to compare yours with mine by following the learning guide that is found in this new edition. I included in my first revision an autobiography focused on my personal life intended to help my readers understand the influences in my life that informed my thinking. Now I turn to a memoir that focuses on my professional life, beginning with my memories and my first book published in 1970 (more than forty years and thirty books ago).

I suspect that I will be 80 by the time this revision is published. It will more than likely be my last revision of what has become my seminal work, the one upon which my career is founded. Before I proceed I would like to thank the many people who chose to learn with me. But mostly I want to dedicate it to Caroline, my wife, without whose support and sacrifices it never would have been completed. An author and educator in her own right, her books, *Calling: A Song For The Baptized, Good Fences: The Boundaries of Hospitality, Transforming the Ordinary,* and *Make All Things New* have informed and inspired me. Together we also have written a number of other books, which will be noted in time.

As long as I can remember I have been on a quest, a quest to develop new questions and therefore discover new answers to explain the phenomena of the Christian faith, its development and transmission. Certainty has never been my goal. Indeed, I have always embraced doubt and its essential place in faith. I contend that the opposite of faith is not doubt, but certainty. I also cherish changing my mind when new questions point to new possible answers.

I have always been more interested in hermeneutics, the interpretations of Scripture, than the content of the Scriptures. I have been more interested in historiography, the history and philosophy of history, than the content of history. I will always remember that every historian brings to her or his writing of history a number of presuppositions, biases, personal values, experiences and perceptions.

I have brought to my quest a passion that is spiritual to its core. While in college I remember holding regular meetings of questioners and doubters in my room to discuss what was not being discussed either at church or in the religion classes offered by the college. My fraternity nickname was "Preach." They joked that I was going to be a preacher, who taught when he preached and preached when he taught. I have always believed that sermons, while a proclamation of the gospel, were also intended to be instructional. My image of a pastor was that of a teacher and teaching was always at the heart of my ministry.

Further, my religious quest was united with a quest to understand why people believed and behaved as they did, that is, how religion and education intersected in the lives of individuals and communities. This explains in part why I chose to study theology at the Harvard Divinity School and work weekends at a Congregational church where the pastor, Dr. Herbert Smith, who had studied law and then theology at Harvard, became my friend and mentor. Harvard in those days was engaged in developing a new curriculum and in securing a totally new and expanded faculty. The academic study of Christianity and other world religions provided an exciting environment for my learning at that time. To this day I can remember fondly every professor with whom I studied and still quote many of their thoughts. My faith, character, and consciousness were significantly formed during these Harvard days and I continue to be grateful for the time and energy the faculty spent in personally guiding my learning.

My decision to be ordained in the Congregational Church (now the United Church of Christ) was in part because in that denomination the pastor was understood to be a teacher and adult learning was a priority. Following ordination my first eight years were spent focused on education. This led me to a call to be a secretary for education at the United Church Board for Homeland Ministries. The United Church in those days hired mavericks and encouraged them to be creative. I gave birth to a magazine named *Colloquy* which initiated a conversation on education in church and society. There were more than twenty of us, socially and theologically liberal, men and women, black and white in this division of the Board. We supported, stimulated, and challenged each other. Beside the magazine I was responsible for all the denominations' congregations on the West Coast, Hawaii and Alaska. I was also our representative to the World Council of Churches and I was a partner in a small consulting and research firm comprised mostly of Harvard education school faculty. Who I have become and what I believe was influenced by the many and diverse experiences that defined my life during these formative years. Later I completed a doctorate at Teachers College, Columbia University in the history and philosophy of education in church and society, with a concentration in cultural anthropology.

The next stop in my pilgrimage was to be Professor of Theology and Christian Nurture at Duke University for more than twenty years. It was a very exciting place. It was a period of reform and renewal. As I remember it, the faculty was particularly close and supportive of each other's scholarly work. Long hours were spent reading each other's articles and conversing in each other's offices. During this time I traveled across the United States and around the world giving lectures. I also wrote many of my books during this period and was for ten years the editor of "Religious Education," the academic journal of the Association of Professors and Researchers in Religious Education. The association was international and included Protestant, Roman Catholic, and Eastern Orthodox Christians and Jews. It also was during this time that I became an Episcopal priest and a new frame of reference developed for my convictions. The consequence of these many interactions and experiences, as I remember them, are best manifested in the many books I wrote during these years. To them I now turn.

Let us begin by tapping my memories of my first book *Values for Tomorrow's Children,* published in 1970. In an introduction, Robert Lynn, Auburn Professor of Religious Education at Union Theological Seminary in New York, and my teacher and friend wrote, "In this book John Westerhoff renews an honorable tradition in American religious literature. He has written a 'tract for our times' at a moment in history when it is sometimes difficult to know where one stands and even more hazardous to assess what is needed for our times. . . . Regretfully in the last decade there has been little if any debate about the coming shape of education in the church. Where now, in the broad mainstream of American Protestantism, can one find a deeply felt argument about our next steps in Christian education. Until now we have had no contemporary equivalent of the arguments over 'nurture and conversion', and of the clash between the proponents of 'progressive religious education' and their neo-orthodox critics. . . . John Westerhoff does not willingly accede to such faint-heartedness, but speaks out of his own 'persuasion' and so addresses all of us as persons capable of caring about faithfulness in the educational work of the church. . . . While I disagree with some of his diagnosis and prognosis, I am ready to begin that important discussion. John Westerhoff is a 'tractarian' suited to the present era. In an interim time between certainties, he has declared himself. Is any body listening? I hope so."

In my preface, I explained that this was not intended to be a scholarly book for academics, but a conversation enabler for every Christian interested in the future of Christian education. It was a consequence of my own struggles. The more I learned about the teaching and learning ministries of the church, the more troubled I became. Why was there so little difference between the lives of baptized Christians who were brought up in the church and those who were not?

It did not appear as if the significant amount time, energy, money and effort spent on the church's educational ministry had made any real difference. I concluded that a Reformation was needed. A Sunday school for children may have once been but was no longer an adequate context for learning to be Christian. I was devoted to shaping an alternative future. *Values for Tomorrow's Children* was to be my first attempt to begin this important conversation.

In preparation for writing this memoir I re-read this small 115-page book I was amazed at how much I still believe, how much its content is still relevant in terms of insights and implications for our contemporary quest, forty years later, to reform the church's educational ministry.

I was interested in how much time I spent being critical of the Sunday School and its instructional methods with children. Nevertheless, I focused mostly on stories of congregations experimenting with alternatives and on the writings of other professionals in the field who had influenced me. Perhaps this explains why many progressive church educators, clergy and laity were so enthusiastic, but also why so many others were highly critical, and branded me as the enemy of the Sunday School. Nevertheless, I was pleased that the conversation had begun and I have been engaged in that conversation ever since. In the ensuing years my fundamental convictions have not changed radically, but I have grown and my thoughts have become deeper and clearer.

My second book, *A Colloquy on Christian Education*, was published two years later, in the closing years of my editorship of "Colloquy." As I remember it, I thought it would be of value to edit a collection of articles I had solicited and published over the years along with some new chapters of my own. I began by once again stating my conviction that we were (I would now say still are) living in an age of transition and an opportunity for a critical turning point in the history of Christianity. We were experiencing a crisis in our understanding of the Christian life of faith, in the nature and character of the church and its relationship to the world; and in the church's teaching and learning ministry. The first eight chapters were foundational, theoretical essays by various scholars who also were friends who have influenced me. The rest of the book was writing by practitioners who told stories of their efforts to take seriously this foundation.

The first article was by Roger Shinn, professor of applied Christianity at Union Theological Seminary in New York. He spoke of education as a mystery (we cannot finally determine our outcomes), but one that requires our intentionality. He explained that Christian education has intellectual content; it is not exclusively a private mystical experience. And it needs to deal not only with theological issues but with the political, economic and social dimensions of our communal lives in church and society.

Next I included an article by Sara Little, a professor at the Presbyterian School of Religious Education in Virginia, one of the very few professional schools devoted to preparing leadership for the church's teaching and learning ministry. Sara reinforced the idea that we now live in a new age calling for new understandings and ways. She contended that three new questions confront us: What is the relationship between the cognitive and the affective, between an intellectual way of thinking and knowing and an intuitive way? Second, what knowledge is of the greatest worth? Third is the question of our ends or goals and being intentional about striving to address them. Here she quotes me: "The end of education must be the welfare of creation and the world community. Education is to serve the purpose of social change, reform, liberation and the humanization of all people rather than maintaining the status quo or the survival of the church."

Phil Phenix, professor of the history and philosophy of education at Teachers College, Columbia University, then explained his conviction that every community of faith seeks to influence the world as well as perpetuate in each new generation the propagation of their faith. But faith, while a consequence of education, does not come by either direct inspiration or some foolproof method of instruction. Faith cannot be taught, it is caught as a result of the influence of social institutions.

An essay by C. Ellis Nelson, professor of practical theology at Union Theological Seminary in New York, followed. Nelson was among my closest friends, teacher and inspiration. He was a soul mate who was also a loving critic. Mostly, I was influenced by his attempt to reestablish the discipline of applied or practical theology and its mission to integrate liturgics and ethics, spirituality and pastoral care, education and the church's mission in the world.

In 1971 I met Gwen Kennedy Neville, a cultural anthropologist interested in theology and socialization or better enculturation theory. She was teaching at Emory University in Atlanta. We were attending a World Council of Churches conference on the world education crisis. After the conference she became my tutor in anthropology. I read every book on her reading lists and more. We exchanged articles we had written for professional journals. Some of these became the content of *Generation to Generation* which marked my first attempt to unite the insights of cultural anthropology to practical theology

Generation to Generation, co-authored with Gwen Kennedy Neville, was born in a transitory period of my life which included time for healing from a car accident, lecturing at Union Theological Seminary in New York and Andover-Newton Theological Seminary in Boston, and a sabbatical year as Lentz Lecturer at Harvard Divinity School. Long conversations with James Fowler of "faith development" fame and Ann Trevelyan, a doctoral student and teaching fellow at the Harvard School of Education in anthropology and education, were of importance to me.

Gwen and I also collaborated on a second book, *Learning Through Liturgy*. I had been inspired by the work of Massey Shepherd an Episcopal liturgiologist and especially by his book

Learning Through Liturgy published in 1965. Gwen took the lead with numerous chapters on anthropology and ritual. Her chapters are followed by mine on the Christian life in liturgical context ending with a long chapter on the practical implications for the church's educational ministry. The insights in this book have been formative in my later studies and in my books written since. What I now believe was indeed a long time coming.

Turning to books that followed, we come first to *Tomorrow's Church* written in 1976. Inspired by my last-century mentor George Albert Coe, I sensed a need for another call to a social understanding of Christian education, an education for social change from a biblical perspective. This small book had a short life span. While appreciated by some, it never spoke to the masses.

Nevertheless, three years later I gave it another try. The result was *Inner Growth—Outer Change: An Educational Guide to Church Renewal*. It was written during another transition time in my life. After twenty years of Christian fellowship and faithful service as a minister in the United Church of Christ, and after a number of years of prayer and discernment, I made the difficult decision to become an Episcopal priest. I will always be grateful for my many years in the United Church. I explain my move to the Episcopal Church as fulfilling a need to unite the Protestant and Catholic in me. During the years that followed, the twenty years I taught practical theology at Duke Divinity School, an ecumenical seminary preparing future clergy for the church, I also worked as a priest at the Chapel of the Cross in Chapel Hill, North Carolina. It became a laboratory for my scholarly work and teaching.

Inner Growth—Outer Change was the result of an ecumenical conference called to consider the need to unite religious experience and prophetic action, deep piety and courageous politics, personal contemplation and social witness. As I put it, "piety without politics is barren, while politics without piety is soulless." As I reread this book, written in turbulent times, I discover a flaw, a flaw in my own theology, a flaw I have attempted to correct recently having been influenced by the *New York Times* correspondent, David Brooks, in his column written on March 20, 2012, entitled "When the Good Do Bad." I have, along with many others, believed that most people were by nature good. I was convinced that I was to look only for the good in people and never give much attention to the fact that there might also be evil in others or myself. Of course, when someone fundamentally good does something evil we are troubled and confused. Now if I'm honest, Christian theology has always asserted that every human being is equally able to be and do both great good and evil. Christian faith historically has envisioned both sinfulness and grace at the center of the human personality. Christian faith has held that we all live in a battlefield between darkness and light, a struggle with the sinful destructive forces within us. Every person, confessed C. S. Lewis, was capable of extraordinary horrors and extraordinary heroism. We are all a mixture of virtue and depravity and our daily task, with God's help, is to strengthen the influence of God's good Holy Spirit and weaken the spirit of evil that, while hidden, is as important as are the influences of heredity and environment. We need to face the fact there is nothing that we are not capable of doing and that resisting the negative aspect of our personality is the responsibility of all the baptized.

Now before we go on, I need to make a diversion to include some other books written during these years. As I have mentioned before, I am not, by nature, a joiner. The church is the only voluntary association to which I have given my full and lifetime devotion. Except for yearly financial contributions, I have never been active in the many alumni groups to which I belong. In fact, most of my friendships have been work oriented. As an introvert I receive the energy I need for inspiration and insight by being alone, reading or meditating. Nevertheless, collaboration has always been important for me. Many of my books were written with another person or were edited volumes comprised of essays by many people whose voices joined mine. I have often taught with another scholar, but I dislike being placed into a small group for reflection. I learn more if I go off alone to contemplate what I have heard or form my own group to ponder some particular issue. Therefore, the associations to which I have belonged were mostly work oriented, for example, the Religious Education Association which I joined in the 1950s. I served on its board of directors and was for a decade editor of its journal "Religious Education." My friends were mostly my colleagues.

I became editor of "Religious Education" on the eve of the Religious Education Association's 75th anniversary. Much had changed over those years and much has changed since then. Believing that an understanding of our history and our interpretation of its meaning are important for contemporary identity and realizing that much had radically changed over these years I edited a book entitled *Who Are We?* comprised of articles published in the journal over the years. The final essay was one of my own, entitled "Risking an Answer."

A few years later I edited another book, this time with O.C. Edwards, onetime president and Dean of Seabury Western Theological Seminary, entitled *A Faithful Church*. Written by some of the church's most insightful historians, these essays trace the history of catechesis, or the church's ministry of teaching and learning, from the early church to the present. I wrote an essay at the beginning and end of the book, the first on "Understanding the Problem" and the last, "Framing and Alternative."

Eight chapters, intended to be scholarly yet for the general public, traced the church's changing understandings of catechesis from the New Testament church through the ancient church, the medieval church, and the protestant reformation church, followed by essays on the Roman Catholic, the Anglican, the eastern orthodox and American church.

My interest in history began during the three years (1955–58) I was studying theology at the Harvard Divinity School where an historical-critical approach to the study of Scripture and tradition dominated. In those days there were no courses on what was called religious education in other seminaries. Nevertheless, I did discover that there was a professor at the School of Education who taught the history and philosophy of education. Robert Ulrich taught a course on religion and education. In his book, *The History of Religious Education* (1968), he wrote, "In a secular society we are inclined to underestimate the role of religion in the history of education. All early education was religious and all early religion was educational." He became a profound influence on my life.

It was Tertullian, the fifth-century bishop of Hippo and theologian, who wrote, "Christians are made not born." That was a very radical idea. Those who accepted this belief in Jesus as the Christ wanted to know how to be disciples. The answer in Greek was "catechesis" literally "to echo," in this case to echo the Word, the Word being a person, Jesus. It was a life-long process of "Christening," that is, influencing the development of Christ-like persons. How that was to be accomplished needed to be related to the ever-changing historical, social, cultural context in which the church found itself. Various methods would emerge to meet changing conditions. It was helpful, therefore, to know the history of the church's many attempts to be faithful and to study its present historical context so as to establish our means. Regretfully *A Faithful Church: Issues in the History of Catechesis* was never popular and the study of the history of catechesis was ignored and therefore the church's vocation to make a Christ-like church comprised of Christ-like persons has been difficult to achieve. When things are going poorly we have a habit of going backward to an imaginary past to establish methods no longer viable, rather than thinking ahead in the light of a realistic past to imagine alternatives. As I pointed out in the end of a *A Faithful Church*, "…in the recent past Protestants developed a Sunday church school as an act of faithfulness while Roman Catholics depended on parochial schools and/or CCD programs similar to Protestant Sunday schools. Both focused the church's teaching and learning ministry, the making of Christians, in terms of instruction in a school setting, a paradigm I have spent my career striving to depreciate."

John Dewey, onetime philosopher of education at Columbia University, who also influenced me, once wrote, "I have learned to take all of my problems back to Plato." I have always believed that familiarity with the past is a necessary resource for understanding the present and imagining the future. So it was that when I pursued a doctorate in education at Columbia Teachers College I wrote my dissertation (now published) on *McGuffey and His Readers: Piety, Morality, and Education in Nineteenth Century America.*

Which brings me to *Schooling Christians,* which I edited with my Duke colleague Stanley Hauerwas. Stanley and I had offices next to each other and were constantly in conversation. Clarity in our thinking was more important than agreement. Neither of us was predictable or consistent. For me the search for truth was founded upon a presupposition concerning truth. Since my early days at Harvard I have contended that truth is keeping two opposite truths in a healthy tension. For example, Jesus is fully human and fully divine. A heresy is a truth gone wild. Example: it is a heresy to believe Jesus is fully human but not fully divine or that Jesus is half human and half divine. In speaking of the truth in any one moment, one may place an emphasis on one dimension of the truth or another, dependent on the situation or the question being addressed. Consider that earlier I identified myself as being a liberal; in *Schooling Christians*, however, I expressed my conservative side which is more dominant. From my perspective, both the liberal and the conservative are necessary if we are to ever approach truth. It is a strange position that is difficult to defend and often results in confusion. For example, I am, in principle, pro-life, but in terms of some particular situations such as rape and incest, pro-choice. I am a defender of capitalism, but I am also a defender of socialism.

Life is paradox; so are truth, goodness and beauty. The church is a human community of Christian faith and the divine incarnate Body of Christ. It is one church, a paradox of the mind: sinful, yet holy, immanent yet transcendent, divided yet one. One day Stanley and I were discussing the growing conviction in some circles that we have reached the moral limits of social liberalism with its understanding of community founded upon the virtue of toleration and its understanding of education founded upon a common school as the necessary crucible for shaping national identity. We thought it would be useful to bring together some of our friends who were also thinking about schooling Christians in a secular, pluralistic, liberal society.

We came up with a list of persons who were struggling with commonness as neutrality along with the conviction that harmony in the social order can be achieved by minimizing or obliterating differences, a melting pot devoid of distinctiveness and uniqueness. With the help of the Lilly Foundation we brought together such a group and *Schooling Christians* was born as we engaged in the many difficult questions about faith and culture in our contemporary era. Our conversations have continued ever since.

Returning to books I have published since the first edition of *Will Our Children Have Faith?* and my personal pilgrimage and the memories of my continuing struggles with the Christian life of faith, I have chosen to begin with that which comprises the Schaff Lectures given at Pittsburg Theological Seminary.

At the time *Building Up God's People in a Materialistic World* was published, I was struggling with a number of issues related to ministry as a profession. While in the past, a profession was related to a personal call from God with a corresponding recognition by the church, in the modern world, a professional was someone who had required the necessary knowledge and skills certified by the academy by a degree (the D.Min. being the highest level of certification for ordained ministry). The seminary also established ministry degrees in areas such as religious education and in other expressions of ministry by the laity that clergy wanted to avoid.

While I personally never experienced a call from God to the priesthood, I did experience the call from the church to be professed in a vow to bear the symbols of priesthood (to bring God to people and people to God), that is, to illumine the priesthood of all the baptized in the church which I discerned prayerfully was also the will of God.

At the same time I was increasingly aware within the discipline of theology, my own area of study, practical or applied theology was comprised of six interrelated dimensions: liturgics (including hermeneutics) and ethics, ascetics (spirituality) and pomoletics (pastoral care), catechetics (formation or nurture, education, and instruction/training) and ecumenics (the church and the world including stewardship and mission, for example). As a practical theologian, my call in recent years has been to be a resident theologian and presbyter in the church, called by the church to prepare future clergy for their roles in the church.

While writing these memoirs, I became painfully aware that most of my life has been divided between a personal life about which my memories are poor and often distorted and a professional life that was clearer and less distorted. Professionally I have devoted my career to the nurture of children (other people's children) in the Christian life of faith; personally I gave the nurture of my children much less attention. Part of that reality was both typical and a product of the age in which I lived. By twenty-one, I had graduated from college, been married and began graduate school. By twenty-four, I had been ordained and begun a span of eight years as a pastor serving three parishes in New England with three children. By thirty, I had bought a home in New Jersey and joined the staff of the United Church Board for Homeland Ministries. It was a very demanding job, with offices in New York and Philadelphia while traveling around the world most of the time. These corresponded to my children's childhood years. By forty, I had completed a second graduate degree and joined the faculty of Duke University, where I wrote *Will Our Children Have Faith?* and four years later *Bringing Up Children in the Christian Faith.* These years corresponded to my children's adolescence.

In the preface to the first edition of *Will Our Children Have Faith?* I wrote, "Aware of my inadequacies as husband and parent, I dedicate this book to my children who have loved me even when I ignored them in my preoccupation with the nurture of other children; and to all parents and children who join me in living by and in God's grace as we strive to live faithfully with each other."

In my early sixties I was divorced and later remarried. I left the university to return to the parish, this time to an Episcopal congregation in Atlanta. Caroline, my present wife, has helped me put my personal and professional life together and as I approach eighty and prepare to retire completely, I find some of my regrettable memories healing. I have experienced forgiveness and I have forgiven myself. I have no need to say more about my personal life. I would prefer to look forward while learning from the past.

While it fits into "do as I say and not as I do", I have discovered that much of my professional life has been filled with wise personal advice I have neglected to follow. While I wish I could begin over I am grateful that God was, in spite of my frailties, able to use me for God's purposes.

My most recent book is *Living Faithfully as a Prayer Book People* (2004). In it I provide a brief history of the Prayer Book and explore how it intends to shape us as a pilgrim and prayerful people. I examine in detail how we Christians can live into our baptism, how we can live a Eucharistic and reconciling life, how our lives can exhibit wholeness, health and well being, and how the spiritual life can aid us to live a holy life in preparation for a holy death.

Two other of my books trace my interest in the role and function of ritual in our life of faith. The first was *Learning Through Liturgy,* written with Gwen Kennedy Neville in 1978 and the second, *Liturgy and Learning Through the Life Cycle,* written two years later with William Willimon, my Duke Divinity School colleague in liturgics and preaching. (He is now a United Methodist Bishop.)

As long as I can remember I have had a passionate concern about religion and ever since college I have been interested in the social sciences: psychology, sociology, anthropology, history, political science and economics. Since my ordination I have added the history and philosophy of education to my list of interests.

Cultural anthropology introduced me to new understandings of symbols, myths and rituals and to faith, character and consciousness. The role of rites and rituals in cultural transmission has particularly interested me. Faith, I have come to believe, is not about beliefs or affirmation of propositional truths, but about perception or "how we see life and our lives." Character is not so much about moral decision-making as it is about interior dispositions, habits of the heart, which unconsciously influence our behavior.

Consciousness is not so much about experience as it is about the awareness that makes experiences possible and help us to understand them. And our rituals, our repetitive, symbolic actions, words and deeds, which express and manifest our community's sacred narrative, are the primary influence in the transmission of our religious community's faith, character and consciousness.

While since the birth of the Christian era, liturgy (our community rituals) and learning have been linked, until recently liturgists and religious educators have gone their separate ways and attempts to reunite them have confused their relationship. Too often educators have spoken of teaching by and with the liturgy thereby reducing liturgy to a didactic act.

Liturgy nurtures the community of faith through celebrative symbolic acts of faith. Catechesis nurtures the community of faith through mindful attempts to communicate and reflect upon the sacred story which underlies and informs these acts of faith.

I can remember the hours I spent in reflecting on the relationship of our communal identity and world-view to our ritual life. I explored how our rituals can either act to bless the way things are (or appear to be) or aid us in critically judging our world-view and value system so that we can be an instrument of cultural change. I discovered that our rituals can also help us escape from reality or to distort that reality. Education (critical reflection on experience) in this case can play a major role in the evaluation and reform of our rituals so as to make them more consistent with our community's life of faith. Most every reform in the history of the church has required a reformation of its rituals and when our rituals change, so do our lives, which explains why liturgical reform is so difficult. Nevertheless, after having explored how ritual and faith are related, I turned to how our rituals affect our spiritual lives, our lives lived

in an ever deepening and loving relationship with God and thereby
with each other.

I further remember that my interests then moved to character
and our life-long initiation into the Christian community of faith
along with the role of ritual in both conversion and nurture. The
result was in the varied books I wrote on the nature and character
of learning and liturgy, of education, rites and rituals.

I can recall the day when Will Willimon and I were discussing
our efforts at Duke to prepare future clergy for the church. One of
our conclusions was that we needed to do a better job in helping
students to integrate their learning and how few text books there
were to aid this effort. We decided to produce a text aimed at this
end. *Liturgy and Learning Through the Life Cycle* was the result
of our efforts. We were aware that it was one thing to argue for a
link between liturgy and learning and another to forge an appropriate link between them. Our challenge was to unite these two
dimensions of practical theology while maintaining their unique
character.

We proceeded to organize our reflections and their possible
implications by first looking at the church's two major sacraments:
baptism and Eucharist. We first discussed these two acts of worship
as major initiating and sustaining, converting and nurturing liturgical events in the church and the lives of its members. We focused
on our new understanding of the significance of baptism and its
essential catechetical complement. We chose to emphasize the lifelong process of living into our baptism and opportunities for confirmation, reception and reaffirmation of our baptismal vows and
covenant. We then explored the church year and our identity as
believers in Jesus Christ and members of his church, his body. We
then turned to our personal and spiritual growth with an emphasis
on daily individual and communal prayer. Next we discussed the
pastoral offices and transitions in our lives: the celebration and
blessing of a marriage and recognition of divorce; thanksgiving for

the birth or adoption of a child, moving and the blessing of a new home, ordination and the celebration of a new ministry and retirement, reconciliation of a penitent, ministration to the sick, ministration at the time of death and the burial of the dead.

Having explored the history, the theology, and the practice of these sacramental occasions, some of them being ancient and others new, we divided each chapter into three parts, the first being a discussion of the history and theology of each specific liturgical act along with an exploration of liturgical norms, such as celebrating baptisms and baptismal renewal at specific times during the church year (such as the Vigil of Easter) and a weekly Eucharistic liturgy that combined word and sacrament. The second section was to be focused on educational or catechetical norms and how they might best relate to each liturgical action such as preparation for the participation in each ceremonial act, the act, and then reflection on our experience in terms of insights and implications for our lives. A third section was to explore norms or directions for the celebration of each rite so that our actions might have the best opportunity of being effective. Our students loved this text and we enjoyed teaching this course together.

As I reflect on these and other memories I have become aware of how I've changed over the years, but also how I have remained the same but deeper in my understandings and convictions. Like all of us, I am to a product of the many influences that have engaged my life. I was born at the end of the first great depression. I am the first person in my family to go beyond high school, earning two doctorates. Due to limited economic resources I had to work my way through college and graduate school. My teachers at Ursinus, Harvard and Columbia had a tremendous influence on me. I still quote them. And I attended the schools I did because of significant scholarship help and the support of others who believed in me when I had to deal with my own low self esteem. I was a young man during the turbulent sixties, with jobs that took me around the globe. I had experiences that led me to an understanding of reconciling justice rather than justice as retribution in which people get what they deserve. The Scriptures have played a major role in my life, but my interpretations of scripture have led me in particular directions; for example, I am convinced that God is biased to the poor, the hungry, the homeless, the oppressed, the sick and dying. I believe that we humans are dependent on God by nature, but God has chosen to be dependent on us. I am convinced that I was made a Saint at my baptism, but I am a Saint who sins and is in need of God's forgiving, reconciling love. I believe that this is God's good world but it is broken and distorts God's will. I have always been a theological and social liberal. The gospel has for me always been a social gospel and our spiritual and moral life is not only personal but communal, political and economic.

Along the way, my fondest memory is finding my soul mate. She too was divorced and worked as a lay person for the Episcopal church. We first met at an Episcopal conference center; she was the convener and I was the speaker. We wrote *On the Threshold of God's Future*. Over twenty one years ago we were married. This has proven to be among the most transformative occasions in my life. But for now, let us return to my memories of writing *On the Threshold of God's Future*. It was conceived during those troubling days in the early 1980s, a time in which most of us were wrestling with a mix of despair, innocence, and hope. We were driven to write this particular book because we both were involved in that age-old love-hate relationship with Christ's church, Christ's body, Christ's presence in this world especially in what we experienced as a threshold time in human history. I remember long and sometimes heated conversations about the church's understanding of its purpose and what it has to offer to our troubled times, especially in terms of the roles of all the baptized, laity and clergy. So it was that this book became a personal testimony to our faith in a God who in spite of all evidence to the contrary always has been and always will be acting to redeem creation in God's due time by transforming evil into good. It is still our conviction that we as members of Christ's body have an obligation to do everything in our power to cooperate with God in the difference he has made and is making in the world.

A few years later I wrote *Living the Faith in Community.* I remember that I was at the time troubled by the fact that the family, for better or worse, was changing; that in our contemporary world the family could never again fulfill the responsibilities it once assumed. While the family, however we define it, will always be a primary context for nurture of children, we can no longer frame a theory of Christian nurture based upon an image of the family or the church from another era in history. I concluded that the church needed to become like a family from the past, a family comprised of multiple generations, a family of families, a community of faith that exists between our ever-changing nuclear families and a society comprised of many institutions and voluntary associations. I was sure of one thing: the family could never be a church nor the church a family. I had no vision of the mega-church which strove to meet all our needs and in the process supported our society's understandings and ways of life. In fact I advocated a church of four hundred active members as being ideal. The church as the Body of Christ was primarily to be a worshipping community of faith that revealed and provided nurture for a social, political, and economic alternative society.

My memories also return to describing in detail the four necessary characteristics of a Christian faith community: The first and perhaps the most important being a common story, sacred narrative or memory and vision. I played out this theme in great detail in another book, *A Pilgrim People,* which took the church year and the assigned gospel texts for each week as the context for retelling and reliving, that is making present again, the church's story. I remember choosing a theological approach to our history by beginning the church story with Good Friday–Easter rather than Advent. I then played out how we might order our church's program, life and ministry according to the story, always returning to the Triduum, the three great days of Holy Week as our referent.

The second characteristic I identified was a common authority which I identified as Scripture, but Scripture that must be interpreted by reason in the light of tradition or the history of changing interpretations. (Historically, Anglican authority was founded upon "Scripture, Reason, and Tradition.") Differences of opinion and changing opinions will result from the application of this authority for our common life which is both inherent and desirable. I am reminded that the opposite of faith is not doubt, doubt being inherent in faith. The opposite of faith is certainty and both liberals and conservatives who are certain of truth as they define it are heretics.

The third characteristic I identified was common rituals, worship or cultic life. This is a recurring theme in all my thought. In this case, I can remember exploring the Greek word for liturgy defined as public service; public service that has two dimensions, namely cultic life and daily life. In theory they are interdependent and affect each other. Nevertheless, our worship and our daily lives can be estranged. I continue to explore the factors leading to this estrangement, aware that if we do not try to unify our liturgical life as being both cultic life and daily life, our communal life of faith will lack authenticity. As I learned first at Harvard that though the church shares religious tasks with many other institutions, the conduct of public worship is its distinctive and unique responsibility. Whenever and wherever persons meet for worship, there is the church. If the church does nothing else for the world, it is doing its greatest service and nothing else it does can compare with that.

And the fourth remembered characteristic of a faith community was a common life together that is more like a communal family than an institution. There will always be institutional elements in the life of a congregation but they must never become dominant, for if they do, stewardship will become church finance and fund raising, evangelism will become church growth and ecumenics will become denominational cooperation. Interestingly, many of my professional colleagues expressed their belief that next to *Will Our Children Have Faith? Living the Faith in Community* is my most important, engaging, provocative and useful book. In 1985 it must have touched a nerve in the lives of those who shared my commitment to the discipline of practical theology. I wish it was still in print.

At this point it might be helpful if I admitted that I have not had many close personal friends in my life. I'm not a joiner. My only community has been my church and my professional colleagues, fellow priests and professors. My self identity is first as a baptized person and then as a pastor and teacher. My wife, Caroline, is my dearest and closest friend. While having many close acquaintances, persons I have considered friends, my dearest male friend is John Eusden who I first met in 1966. When we first met we were both ministers in the United Church of Christ. I was "pastor and teacher" of the First Congregational Church in Williamstown Mass. He was chaplain and professor at Williams College and a member of First Church. During the ensuing years we went in different directions. He continued as a professor at Williams but shifted his academic interests from New England church history to world religions and environmental studies. One dimension of our lives which remained constant was a common search for a spiritual life that would draw us into an ever-deepening and loving relation with God. I had gone on my search by turning to the history of the Christian church: Eastern Orthodox, Roman Catholic, and Protestant (mostly Anglican). He turned to Eastern religions, particularly Taoism and Mahayana Buddhism. During the 80s our friendship was reborn and it has grown ever since, even though we do not see each other often anymore. I will always remember, however, those days of walking the beach or hiking a trail in which we shared our spiritual pilgrimages. Those conversation resulted in *The Spiritual Life: Learning East and West.*

In the writing of that book I became increasingly aware that after becoming fully familiar and knowledgeable of one's own faith and religion in its diversity (for example Christianity East and West), it is important that we immerse ourselves experientially and reflectively in the practice and thought of at least one other world religion. In my journey I have sought to better understand Hinduism, Buddhism, Judaism and Islam. In the process, I have become more familiar and devoted to my own Christian faith and more sure of my particular slant on the Christian life of faith. In our retirement and struggling with aging, John and I have begun a last book whose working title is the *Human Quest for Wholeness, Health and Well-being.*

Now over a decade ago, while teaching at Duke, I remember becoming aware of the need for academic courses in both the spiritual life and spiritual formation through intentional experiences that would contribute to the growth and development of the spiritual life. At first this concern was shared by only a few students and faculty, but before I left Duke a spiritual formation program had been established. My foundation course was being taken by most students in their first year, other courses that dealt with the spiritual life were offered and there were plans to hire a professor of spirituality.

I also well remember that in my last years at Duke I experienced a crisis in my own life which led me to realize that even though I had a spiritual discipline and had been teaching courses on the spiritual life, my own was in disarray. While continuing to teach, I became an associate of the Society of Saint John, the Evangelist, an Anglo-Catholic men's religious order. I lived with and shared in their common life at St. John's House in Durham, North Carolina. I started seeing a spiritual director and participating in the Rite of Reconciliation weekly. Along the way I participated in a thirty-day Ignatian Retreat to aid my discernment on what God wanted me to do next with my life.

These experiences led me to the conviction that if I was to continue to be a practical theologian I needed to leave the academe and return to the parish to become an educational resource for both laity and clergy. I had a dream of birthing a parish-based Institute for Pastoral Studies. Therefore, following my marriage to Caroline, I moved to Atlanta where she was the bishop's canon for ministry. I was invited to house my Institute at St. Bartholomew's in Atlanta while I continued to fly back and forth to Duke until I could complete my discernment. During that year the rector of St. Bartholomew's was called to be Dean at a Cathedral and I became interim rector. During this period, I concluded I was doing what God wanted me to do and I moved to St. Luke's in Atlanta to continue my work as director of the Pastoral Studies Institute, theologian in residence, and priest associate for liturgy and learning.

I remember my discovery that lay people were asking questions about spiritual life and its relationship to their work and parenthood. Clergy complained about "burn out" and having nothing left to give, and that returning to the seminary for continuing education didn't satisfy their deeper needs. Others complained about "drain out." What they admitted they suffered from was "rustout" from ignoring their spiritual lives. *The Spiritual Life: The Foundation of Preaching and Teaching* was written to meet that need. Interestingly, this book became the major study book for the chaplains in the Armed Forces.

After eight years in the parish, eight years as a denominational executive, twenty years in the academy, and ten years directing an

Institute, I retired only to become part-time priest and resident theologian in St. Anne's Episcopal Church in Atlanta. During all these years I wrote numerous books and lectured around the world. I was pleased that Church Publishing suggested we republish my revised edition of *Will Our Children Have Faith?* and add a memoir that puts my life and work in context. I am grateful for this opportunity, but I must include one more book and the memories and vision that surround it. That book is *Sensing Beauty,* written with my friend John Eusden. It is a book about aesthetics, the human spirit and the church and it attempts to address the relationship between beauty, truth and goodness. It best describes my current convictions about many things, including my quest for a practical theology in our day.

For a number of years now I have been in search of an historicist perspective to understanding the human being and our understandings of human life. In doing so, I have found it useful to identify the age of faith from the 10th to the 16th centuries, the so called Middle Ages, in which the intuitive way of thinking and knowing was dominant. Then after a period of time this era ended and a new era was born, namely the age of reason in which the intellectual way of thinking and knowing became dominant. This so called enlightenment era has now moved into a technological age and I would argue that we are becoming aware of the moral limits of making reason and the sciences dominant.

This is not to deny the many important discoveries made during this era nor is it to say that cultivating the imagination has not played a significant role in these discoveries. For me, the issue is the fact that we have depreciated the role of the arts (dance, music, drama, literature, poetry and the visual arts) in our understandings of human nature. In *Sensing Beauty,* we defined beauty as the revelation of the presence of goodness and truth (priestly art) and the revelation of the absence of goodness and truth (prophetic art). In both cases, revelation (in contrast to reason) is dominant in our search for truth and goodness. This helps me understand the growth of two movements in terms of reason. The first is atheism, which makes the intellect supreme, and the charismatic or Pentecostal movement, which has a tendency toward anti-intellectualism and makes feelings supreme. What I believe the church needs to do is to be counter-cultural and provide an alternative by focusing on revelation and the intuitive way of thinking and knowing and on the imagination and the role of the arts in the life of the church. Reason will continue to play a role in our attempts to reflect on our experiences and understand both their meaning and their implication for our lives. But the imagination and revelation will play a dominant role in the experiences we nurture and provide in our communal life, prayer, and worship. Nurture or formation comes first, but education and intellectual reflection on experience need to play a role.

From the beginnings of humanity the relationship between the arts and religion has been debated. Separation and remarriage have been one important aspect of their history. Both make claims about their role in revelation (a revealing of that which is true but hidden and can only be discovered by the intuition and imagination). It further appears that people are more convinced by the arts and what they perceive to be true than by cognitive logical argument or rhetoric. And we need to remember that the imagination involves our response to the revelatory nature of the arts and religion. Recall the words of Augustine at the Eucharist: "Be what you see. Receive who you already are." Faith understood as perception is not irrational nor is it fired by undisciplined whim and fancy. It uses all the facilities of the mind in its search for truth, meaning and purpose. The imagination and creativity are primary instincts in human beings. Only if the intuition and the affections are taken seriously will persons be able to have experiences in teaching, learning and worship that make faith understood as perception possible. This implies that it is not enough to teach the history and philosophy of the arts. We need to encourage participation in the arts for all people (children, youth, and adults) and not just those who have made the arts a career choice. I would go so far as to argue that the arts provide the core around which the curriculum of Christian education must be built and from which other curricular concerns be derived.

The problem with the age of reason into which we have been enculturated is that it has permitted a wedge to be driven between subjective experience and objective reflection, between the intuition and the intellect, between the sacred and the profane, between revelation and theology.

As I bring this memoir to a close I am reminded of a biblical narrative noted by Parker Palmer in his book *To Know as We Are Known,* in which he explains that teaching and learning typically rely on factual observation and logical cognitive analysis which deny and/or neglect the role of the arts in human knowing.

In the biblical myth of Adam and Eve we have an account of the first sin, which is an epistemological distortion. Adam and Eve are driven from the garden, a place of harmony and communion not because they sought knowledge but because they sought a particular kind of knowledge. They sought knowledge that excluded God, mystery, awe and wonder. They sought objective knowledge that would put them in charge, independent and in control, a power belonging to God alone.

During the years I have left I intend to devote myself to influencing a change in our understanding of a Christian education, an education that focuses on the intuition, the imagination, the performing arts, revelation, and experience. Will our children have faith? Only if we adults have faith and share it with our children through our participation with them in the performing arts in the church. Let us never forget that if we care about the next generation we will worry about our own. The place to begin is with ourselves. Only then will we have a chance to bring up our children in the Christian faith.

Study Guide

by Sharon Ely Pearson

First written in 1976, *Will Our Children Have Faith?* was a prophetic voice and call to the Christian community to take back religious education that had been relegated entirely to Sunday morning classes for children. John Westerhoff called the church to move beyond teaching children the facts about religion, to learning and experiencing what it means to be a faithful Christian. Since then, the church has acknowledged the need for critical reflection on the Christian faith and life in the light of Scripture, tradition, reason and reflection on experience. However, almost forty years after it was first published, we still need to ask the question Dr. Westerhoff posed in the revised edition (2000): "How are we who are believers in Jesus Christ and the members of his church to live?"

Dr. Westerhoff brought back the concept of holistic learning in what it means to be formed in faith as a Christian. Today, the term "Christian formation" is increasingly accepted as embracing the six dimensions of study that had once been separated. While the term "catechesis" has not been as widely accepted in our common language in the Protestant educational arena, it is recognized that liturgy (including homiletics), pastoral care, ethics, spirituality, stewardship, evangelism, mission and ministry have joined with education as a practical discipline that encompasses Christian formation. Education continues to remain the key to faithful, intentional formation.

Today we speak of formation, discipleship, mentoring and practice as well as education in our churches. For those involved in the ministry of Christian formation, there is the understanding that a Christian is one who is on a lifelong journey, a pilgrimage engaging our body, mind and spirit as we seek to know and be known to God. But is anyone listening?

The first decade of this twenty-first century witnessed a slow, overall erosion of the strength of America's congregations, according to the *Faith Community Today* series of national surveys of American congregations. If one attends church regularly, that might mean only once a month. Many no longer affiliate with a particular denomination, although still calling themselves "Christian." Most congregations have an average worship attendance of less than 125 per week. Technology and globalization have had an impact on the church, too. The FACT series shows that the decade brought:

- A continued increase in innovative, adaptive worship
- A surprisingly rapid adoption of electronic technologies
- A dramatic increase in racial/ethnic congregations, many for immigrant groups
- A general increase in the breadth of both member-oriented and mission-oriented programs

FACT also gave witness to an increase in connection across faith traditions, but a steep drop in financial health, continuing high levels of conflict, and aging memberships. The net, overall result: fewer persons in the pews and decreasing spiritual vitality. In *American Religion: Contemporary Trends* (Princeton University

Press, 2011), Mark Chavez discovered that most Americans say they believe in God, and more than a third say they attend religious services every week. Yet the statistics show that people do not really go to church as often as they claim, and it is not always clear what they mean when they say they believe in God or pray. Only 9% of Americans in 2008 said that religion was the most important thing in their life (Putnam and Campbell, *American Grace: How Religion Divides and Unites Us*, 2010).

Theologian and church historian Diana Butler Bass is one of many who describe today as a post-Christian society. Many adults no longer speak a Christian "language" or engage in faith practices that shape their personal or family life. In *Process not Program – Adult Faith Formation for Vital Churches* (Alban Institute, 2011) she says, "Christian illiteracy in a post-Christian society is a daily reality. As leaders, we are learning to assume no theological knowledge or Christian practice. And even many of our long-term church members are seeking to go deeper, find connections in life and faith, explore vocational and career concerns, and ask hard questions about the Bible, ethics, and world religions."

With the large group of baby boomers (born between 1946 and 1964) now entering their 60s, we are seeing the membership of our churches aging. What is happening to post-boomer generations? Numerous studies (including *The National Study of Youth and Religion*) of youth and young adults have shown the importance of spirituality in the lives of young people continues to increase, while at the same time the importance of participating in religious organizations has declined somewhat. The role of faith in the lives of their parents is also instrumental in how they practice their faith.

It is with today's context in mind that we re-enter Dr. Westerhoff's *Will Our Children Have Faith?*, listening to that still-prophetic voice for today and tomorrow's children.

Chapter One: The Shaking of Foundations

No longer can we assume that the educational understandings that have informed us, or the theological foundations that have undergirded our efforts, are adequate for the future. A continuing myopic concern for education, understood primarily as schooling and instruction and undergirded by increasingly vague pluralistic theologies, will not be adequate for framing the future of religious education. Today we face an extremely radical problem which only revolution can address. We must now squarely face the fundamental question: Will our children have faith? (p. 2)

1. What is your current Christian education program modeled after: the schooling-instructional paradigm or a holistic ecology of a community that reflects on the meaning and significance of life? What would it take to move to a new ecology of formation?

2. How is your Christian education program planned in light of the total mission and ministry of your church?

3. In what ways can your congregation ground its educational ministries in the Christian faith through nurture in a worshipping, witnessing community of faith?

4. How does your educational programming offer the five levels of "thinking and knowing" (knowing, comprehension, application, analysis, synthesis and evaluation) that Dr. Westerhoff summarizes in his 2000 update to this chapter? (p. 22) What areas need strengthening in your setting?

Chapter Two: Beginning and Ending with Faith

Education as action/reflection can play a significant role in helping us to live, individually and corporately, under the judgment and inspiration of the Gospel to the end that God's will be done and God's community (kingdom) comes . . . To respond to that call is to decide what issues must be addressed and hence emphasized. (p. 30)

1. Dr. Westerhoff lists a theological framework that he believes is most crucial for the church's educational mission and ministry. Do you agree? What is missing? What order of importance would you put them in?

   a. The nature of God – revelation and authority

   b. The nature of persons – conversion and nurture

   c. The nature of church – discipleship and individual-social life

2. What is the place and role of scripture in teaching children, youth and adults in your congregation? Does it serve as a "textbook" and focus of your educational ministry? How does your congregation, as a community and as individuals, read and interpret scripture?

3. The Episcopal Church has a document entitled *The Children's Charter for the Church.* A portion of it states that the church is called:

   a. to receive, nurture and treasure each child as a gift from God;

   b. to proclaim the Gospel to children, in ways that empower them to receive and respond to God's love;

    c. to give high priority to the quality of planning for children and the preparation and support of those who minister with them;

    d. to include children, in fulfillment of the Baptismal Covenant, as members and full participants in the Eucharistic community and in the church's common life of prayer, witness and service.

How does your church nurture its members, including children?

4. In our post-Christian society, claiming the name "Christian" takes on new meaning. How is your church a unique witnessing community of faith? How does worship inspire and motivate individuals to join God in God's work of peace, justice and reconciliation in the world?

5. How does your commitment to faith, character and consciousness influence how you and your church engage in educational ministry?

Chapter Three: In Search of Community

If our children are to have faith, we need to make sure that the church becomes a significant community of faith. To meet this challenge we need to take seriously the characteristic of community and we need to examine, evaluate, plan, and develop educational programs around three aspects of corporate life: the rituals of the people; the experiences persons have within the community; and the actions members of the community perform, individually and corporately, in the world. (pp. 53–54)

1. Who are the teachers in your community? The prophets? The apostles?

2. What roles does liturgy play in teaching and passing on faith in your congregation? Discuss the ways your community practices:

a. Rites of community

b. Life crisis rites

3. How are children a part of your worshipping community? Are they present? Why or why not? What roles do they play in leadership and participation?

4. How is your congregation a praying community? How can this be strengthened?

5. In what ways do you help persons regain their God-given ability to wonder and create; to dream and fantasize; imagine and envision; to sing, paint, dance and act?

6. How do you help others acquire the skills necessary to be responsible political and social activists in proclaiming the Gospel in their daily life and vocation?

7. Does your community value diversity? In what outward and visible ways?

Chapter Four: Life Together

Until adults in the church are knowledgeable in their faith, have experienced the transforming power of the Gospel, live radical lives characteristic of the disciples of Jesus Christ, no new curriculum, no new insights on learning, no new teacher-training programs, and no new educational technology will save us. (p. 86)

1. How do you help your members answer the questions Dr. Westerhoff poses:

a. How can I be what I say I am?

b. How can I live what I profess?

2. How would you describe experienced faith, affiliative faith, searching faith and owned faith? Where do you find yourself

within these concentric circles? Do you agree with this
generalization of styles of faith? Why or why not?

3. Name your own experiences (or those of others) that have
occurred at each of these styles. Are there milestones that can
be attributed to each?

4. Do you agree that few adults have an owned faith? Why or
why not?

5. What kinds of opportunities and experiences do you provide
children, youth and adults to help them move from one style
of faith to another?

6. How does Dr. Westerhoff's updated "paths" of pilgrimage
on a faith journey (experiential way, reflective way and
integrative way) compare to his previous "styles of faith"?

7. Review the faith development models of James Fowler, James
Loder and Gabriel Moran. How are these similar or different
to the models given here?

Chapter Five: Hope for the Future

*Our children will have faith if we have faith and are faithful. Both
we and our children will have Christian faith if we join with others
in a worshiping, learning, witnessing Christian community of faith.
(p. 126)*

1. Define the educational ministry for your congregation.

2. How can you evaluate and plan your formation programs
in an integral way as described in this chapter, given the
examples shown?

3. What are the principles used for your adult religious
education? How might you follow the principles given here:

      a. Go where they are

      b. Focus on questions, problems and needs that are shared

      c. Offerings are five weeks or shorter

      d. Begin where the participants are

      e. Be action and outcome focused

4. How is faith being formed in your congregation today?

5. Discuss all aspects of formation in your congregation, including the preparation of persons for baptism, communion and confirmation. Reflect on other aspects of formal and informal learning that is happening.

6. How comprehensive are the offerings for children, youth and adults in the many aspects of liturgy, ethics, spirituality, pastoral care and witness in addition to traditional instructional and educational models?

Afterword

Formation is best understood as the participation in and the practice of the Christian life of faith. It is a process of transformation and formation, of conversion and nurture. (p. 142)

Evaluate the areas of formation in which the whole life of the congregation forms Christians in either positive or negative ways:

1. Ritual participation – the gathering together for worship in all its forms

2. The environment – all that we see, taste, touch, smell and hear as well as the arrangement of space in which we gather

3. The ordering of time – our faith, character and consciousness are shaped by the organization of the Church's calendar based on our salvation story

4. The organization of the communities life together – equipping the saints for ministry in daily life and work

5. Communal interactions – how life in the congregation is a sign to the world of what life in God's reign looks like

6. Role models – those persons, past and present, whom we raise up to be examples of some aspect of the Christian life

7. Disciplines – the practices of prayer and caring for others

8. Language – being intentional in how we talk, being conscious of racist or sexist remarks and the oppression of others

The Charter for Lifelong Christian Formation

Dr. Westerhoff believes that children will have faith if the adults who surround them have faith. In 2009, The Episcopal Church adopted *The Charter for Lifelong Christian Formation* as a means to lift up the importance of adult faith formation. You will discover the language of The Charter resonates with the language and vision described in *Will Our Children Have Faith?*

Through The Charter, we are *invited* to a life of prayer, service, education and worship; *inspired* to experience our faith journey through the lens of worship, scripture, reason and tradition; and are *transformed* to live into our baptismal promises, serving, witnessing, empowering and holding all accountable.

The Charter provides an intentional opportunity to plan and support our lifelong formation. It provides a framework for dioceses to organize their formation ministries and programs. Faith formation for people of all ages informs, forms and transforms people and communities by providing an encounter with Christ and promoting discipleship.

- *To inform,* we impart knowledge of the Christian faith so that who we are and how we live is shaped and influenced by what we know.
- *To form,* we nurture people's identity and lifestyle as disciples of Christ.
- *To transform,* we promote the personal and social transformation of the world according to the kingdom of God that Jesus preached.

The Charter allows us to engage all generations in more active participation in church life; to equip and support families, especially parents, to practice the Christian way of life at home and in their daily lives; to transform the church community into a community of lifelong learners; and to utilize the whole life of the church as the faith formation curriculum through church year, feasts and seasons, sacraments and liturgy, justice and service, prayer and spirituality, and community life.

The premises of Christian formation – holistic integration of learning, the importance of context, the need for interdependence and cooperation, and the value of relationships and dialogue – all inform how we conduct the Church's mission. Mission then involves sharing stories as well as building hospitals, social transformation as well as personal service.

An important part of being Christian in a multi-faith society is to understand one's faith enough to be able to live in the world honoring that faith while honoring and affirming others' faith. Christian formation and theological education courses are essential to instilling that deep understanding and knowledge to empower Christians to be able to say what they believe in.

How might this document help you frame your adult formation vision in your congregation?

The Charter for Lifelong Christian Formation

*(adopted at the 76th General Convention of
The Episcopal Church, 2009)*

Lifelong Christian Faith Formation in The Episcopal Church
is Lifelong growth in the knowledge, service and love of God as
followers of Christ and is informed by Scripture, Tradition and
Reason.

I have called you friends. John 15:14-16

Through the Episcopal Church, God *Invites* all people:
- To enter into a prayerful life of worship, continuous
  learning, intentional outreach, advocacy and service.
- To hear the Word of God through scripture, to honor
  church teachings, and continually to embrace the joy of
  Baptism and Eucharist, spreading the Good News of the
  risen Christ and ministering to all.
- To respond to the needs of our constantly changing
  communities, as Jesus calls us, in ways that reflect our
  diversity and cultures as we seek, wonder and discover
  together.
- To hear what the Spirit is saying to God's people, placing
  ourselves in the stories of our faith, thereby empowering us
  to proclaim the Gospel message.

*You did not choose me, but I chose you and
appointed you to go and bear fruit.*

John 15:14-16

Through the Episcopal Church, God *Inspires* all people:

- To experience Anglican liturgy, which draws us closer to God, helps us discern God's will and encourages us to share our faith journeys.

- To study Scripture, mindful of the context of our societies and cultures, calling us to seek truth anew while remaining fully present in the community of faith.

- To develop new learning experiences, equipping disciples for life in a world of secular challenges and carefully listening for the words of modern sages who embody the teachings of Christ.

- To prepare for a sustainable future by calling the community to become guardians of God's creation.

I am giving you these commands
that you may love one another.

John 15:17

Through The Episcopal Church, God *Transforms* all people:

- By doing the work Jesus Christ calls us to do, living into the reality that we are all created in the image of God and carrying out God's work of reconciliation, love, forgiveness, healing, justice and peace.

- By striving to be a loving and witnessing community, which faithfully confronts the tensions in the church and the world as we struggle to live God's will.

- By seeking out diverse and expansive ways to empower prophetic action, evangelism, advocacy and collaboration in our contemporary global context.

- By holding all accountable to lift every voice in order to reconcile oppressed and oppressor to the love of God in Jesus Christ our Lord.

Christian Faith Formation in The Episcopal Church
is a lifelong journey
with Christ, in Christ, and to Christ.

Sharon Ely Pearson is the Christian Formation Specialist for Church Publishing Incorporated with over 30 years of experience in ministry with children, youth and adults on the congregational, diocesan and church-wide level. She received an MACE from Virginia Theological Seminary and is the co-author of *The Prayer Book Guide to Christian Education, 3rd edition* (Morehouse, 2009) and *Call on Me: A Prayer Book for Young People* (Morehouse, 2012). She is a member of The Episcopal Church's Standing Commission on Lifelong Christian Formation and Education.

Other Books by John H. Westerhoff

1970   *Values for Tomorrow's Children*

1972   *A Colloquy on Christian Education* (editor)

1974   *Generation to Generation* (with Gwen Kennedy Neville)

1975   *Tomorrow's Church*

1976* *Will Our Children Have Faith?*

1977   *McGuffey and His Readers: Piety, Morality & Education in 19th Century America*

1978   *Who Are We? The Quest for a Religious Education* (editor)

1978   *The Church's Ministry in Higher Education* (editor)

1978   *Learning Through Liturgy* (with Gwen Kennedy Neville)

1979   *Inner Growth—Outer Change*

1979   *Christian Believing* (with Urban Holmes)

1979   *Bringing Up Children in the Christian Faith*

1980* *Liturgy & Learning Through the Life Cycle* (with Will Willimon)

1980   *A Faithful Church: Issues on the History of Catechesis* (editor with O.C. Edwards)

1981   *The Spiritual Life: Learning East and West* (with John Eusden)

1982   *Building God's People*

1983   *A Pilgrim People*

1984   *Living the Faith Community*

1985   *On the Threshold of God's Future* (with Caroline Hughes)

1989* *Living Into Our Baptism* (with Caroline Hughes)

1989   *Planning for Education Within Congregations* (with Caroline Hughes)

1993   *Schooling Christians* (edited with Stanley Hauerwas)

1994*   *The Spiritual Life: The Foundation for Preaching and Teaching*

1994*   *To Teach and Learn: A Catechist Guide for the Episcopal Church*

1995*   *A People Called Episcopalians: A Resource for Inquiry Classes*

1996*   *Holy Baptism: A Guide for Parents and Godparents*

1997*   *Grateful & Generous Hearts: A Resource for Stewardship*

1998*   *To Love and to Cherish, Till Death Do Us Part: A Guide for Marriage Preparation*

1998*   *Sensing Beauty* (with John Eusden)

2004*   *Living Faithfully as a Prayer Book People*

*in print 2012